Here's what people are saying ab[...]

"I so appreciate this book—it is full of hea[...] to remind us of God's faithfulness, even in our failures. God is still an awesome God, and Dee and Lori celebrate this!"

—SANDI PATTY, INSPIRATIONAL SINGER

"I was captivated by *My Daughter, My Daughter*. Every Christian woman will be challenged by the remarkable story of how God called one woman who responded with obedience when He gave her an impossible mission. *My Daughter, My Daughter* has the rare combination of a riveting story and an extraordinary Bible study all in one book. This could forever change your life. Don't miss this book!"

—CAROL KENT, SPEAKER AND AUTHOR

"The weaving together of contemporary and biblical examples of women who faced real-life issues encourages me. Coupling this with a hands-on Bible study challenges me to dig out God's truth for my own life situations. I think this is a great book—you will not want to put it down!"

—RUTH GRAHAM MCINTYRE, SPEAKER, AUTHOR,
DAUGHTER OF RUTH AND BILLY GRAHAM

"Having grown up under the influence of godly grandmothers and mother, I have a real appreciation for the heritage they have passed down to me. It has been such a privilege to be a part of the Heritage Keepers conferences and to see the heart of Bob and Lori Beckler. Those who read *My Daughter, My Daughter* will be as encouraged as I am to share the message of God's love for us."

—DENISE JONES, POINT OF GRACE

"*My Daughter, My Daughter* is what all we grown-up little girls long to hear—a deeply personal invitation to walk into a Father's embrace, in whatever state we happen to be in. Written with wisdom, vulnerability, and beauty, this book will bless the deepest longings of any woman's heart. Dee Brestin has captured the miracle of Heritage Keepers and mingled it with compelling real-life stories and comforting, biblical truth. A treasure!"

—BECKY FREEMAN, NATIONAL SPEAKER, AUTHOR

"*My Daughter, My Daughter* presents biblical evidence that the truth of God's Word is both illuminating and directing, and that the love in God's Word is wooing and connecting.... It offers both motivation and celebration."

—DR. ROSEANNE COLEMAN, NATIONAL SPEAKER AND
PRESIDENT OF ROSEANNE COLEMAN MINISTRIES, INC.

"Women are called to so many tasks—from fixing the faucet to settling squabbles to nuturing the needy. Yet the greatest call of all is to pass on our holy heritage to the next generation. Deuteronomy 6:6 calls us to talk about the things of the Lord when we sit at home, when we walk along the road, and when we lie down and get up. *My Daughter, My Daughter* will equip you to answer this holy call."

—LYNDA HUNTER, EDITOR, FOCUS ON THE FAMILY

Heritage Keepers recommends the following books and guides
by Dee Brestin for individual or small group use:

The Friendships of Women

The Friendships of Women Workbook

We Are Sisters

The Joy of Women's Friendships

The Joy of Eating Right

The Joy of Hospitality

A Woman of Joy

A Woman of Value

A Woman of Insight

A Woman's Journey Through Luke

A Woman's Journey Through Ruth

A Woman's Journey Through Esther

A Woman's Journey Through 1 Peter

A six minute promotional video on *My Daughter, My Daughter* is available to you
at minimal cost through Heritage Keepers. It features exciting footage of
Point of Grace, Kathy Troccoli, Sandi Patty, Dee, and Lori. This can be used to
interest women in studying *My Daughter, My Daughter* in small groups. Call
Heritage Keepers or order through their website.

For more information on Heritage Keepers Conferences
call 1-800-497-2660,
or see www.HeritageKeepers.com

Dee's books are available at your local Christian bookstore or from
Chariot Victor Publishing, 800-437-4337.

My Daughter My Daughter

Chariot Victor Publishing
A Division of Cook Communications

Chariot Victor Publishing,
a division of Cook Communications, Colorado Springs, Colorado 80918
Cook Communications, Paris, Ontario
Kingsway Communications, Eastbourne, England

MY DAUGHTER, MY DAUGHTER

Printed in the United States of America.

2 3 4 5 6 7 8 9 10 Printing/Year 03 02 01 00

Editor: Lee Hough, Julie Smith
Design: Keith Sherrer

Library of Congress Cataloging-in-Publication Data
Brestin, Dee
        My daughter, my daughter/by Dee Brestin and Lori Beckler.
            p. cm.
        ISBN 1-56476-784-1
        1. Christian women--Religious life.   I. Beckler, Lori.
II. Title.
BV4527.B695   1999   99-39736
248.8'43--dc21   CIP

Contents

Dedication

Dee dedicates this book to
her daughter-in-law, Julie Brestin,
who is more like a beloved daughter,
and to her powerful prayer team

Lori dedicates this book to
her parents and grandparents,
the Becklers and the Bowlings, and to the
Heritage Keepers' friends and family

---

*Because of your faithfulness,
the next generation will know*

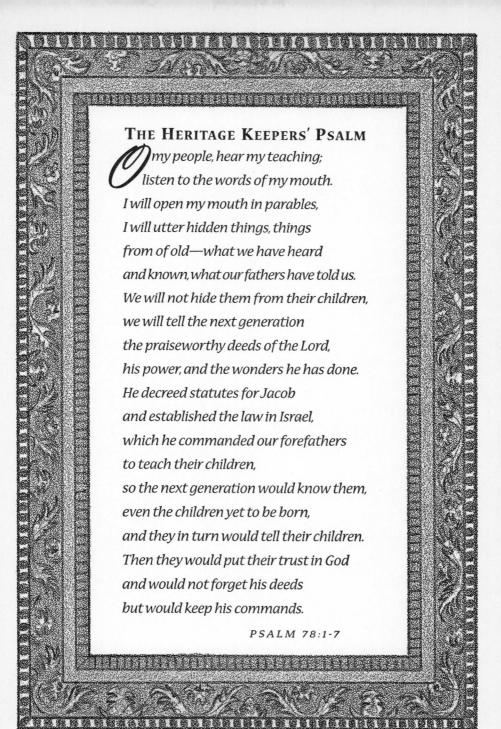

THE HERITAGE KEEPERS' PSALM

O my people, hear my teaching;
listen to the words of my mouth.
I will open my mouth in parables,
I will utter hidden things, things
from of old—what we have heard
and known, what our fathers have told us.
We will not hide them from their children,
we will tell the next generation
the praiseworthy deeds of the Lord,
his power, and the wonders he has done.
He decreed statutes for Jacob
and established the law in Israel,
which he commanded our forefathers
to teach their children,
so the next generation would know them,
even the children yet to be born,
and they in turn would tell their children.
Then they would put their trust in God
and would not forget his deeds
but would keep his commands.

PSALM 78:1-7

Acknowledgments

We give thanks for and ask God's blessings upon:

Our prayer team, who has prayed through every step of this book. Often we have felt the warm breath of the Lion of Judah on our necks, and we know that is because of your faithfulness in prayer.

The friends and family of Heritage Keepers, without whom this book would not be. You have given sacrificially of your time, energy, and money.

Gay Tillotson, Dee's assistant, who has given the last nine months of her life to help produce this baby, and has cared for it tenderly and conscientiously.

Point of Grace and their mothers, for providing such a wonderful example of passing on the heritage.

Kathy Troccoli and her friends, Allyson Baker, Ellie Lofaro, and Pamela Muse, for their gracious and insightful interviews.

Sandi Patty, for her graciousness, her willingness to obey God, and her church, the North Anderson Church of God, for supporting her, and giving her, as she says, "a safe place to heal and confront myself."

The Chariot Victor team, for being a catalyst for this book, particularly to our insightful editor, Julie Smith, and to Lee Hough, for believing in the message of Heritage Keepers.

Our husbands, Steve Brestin and Bob Beckler, who have stood by us, prayed for us, counseled us, and cheered us on.

Lori's children, Nicole and Daniel Beckler, for their dedication, sacrifice, and prayers for Heritage Keepers, and Dee's daughters still at home, Beth and Anne Brestin, for their love and grace.

One

Listen, O daughter,
consider and give ear.

PSALM 45:10a

My Daughter,
My Daughter

*A*s we move deeply into the twenty-first century, I believe we will look back to the 1990s and recognize the historical signs of *revival*. Revival occurs when God bends down and calls to His children, His sons and His daughters, and revives them with His Spirit. The story I am going to tell you involves a women's conference called Heritage Keepers, but it is broader than that, for the message God gave to those founding Heritage Keepers is a message He seems to be whispering to His daughters everywhere.

MARKET SQUARE ARENA: INDIANAPOLIS, INDIANA, SEPTEMBER 20, 1997

As thousands of excited women poured into Market Square Arena in Indianapolis, two contrasting figures stood in the shadows watching: Wellington Boone, the fiery black preacher from Promise Keepers, and Lori Beckler, the soft-spoken wife and mother who first sensed God's call for Heritage Keepers. Wellington shook his head in amazement at the crowd and said:

"The networking you must have done! Just how many pastors did you contact, woman?"

Lori laughed softly. "None."

"What?" Wellington raised his bushy eyebrows.

Lori shook her blond head. "We didn't network. We prayed."

"Well, where did you advertise, Lori? *Today's Christian Woman?* *Guideposts?* The *Indianapolis Star?"*

"We advertised on the radio, Wellington. But no major print ads. We didn't have the money for that."

"No ads in the major magazines? None in the paper?"

"No, Wellington," Lori repeated. "We prayed."

Wellington stared at Lori, his eyes wide, his mouth open in aston-ishment. Lori's own eyes were filling with tears. Wellington raised his hands to heaven and exclaimed: **"This is the mighty hand of God!"**

Heritage Keepers is just one of many large women's conferences that followed in the wake of Promise Keepers. The story of the founding of Heritage Keepers is an exciting faith story, a writer's dream, but one that has strengthened my own walk with God tremendously. As I interviewed Lori and many of the gifted artists who sensed a call to Heritage Keepers, their stories affirmed to me again that we belong to a God who is personal, who bends down and calls to His daughters. You will read how:

God seemed to whisper to Lori Beckler, calling her to change from booking conferences for the world to booking conferences for Him.

God seemed to bring Lori and her husband to their knees, broken, in April of 1997, when it looked like they might lose their home and their parents' retirement savings because of their investment in Heritage Keepers.

God seemed to compel the agent for Point of Grace to call at the above critical moment.

God seemed to prompt Kathy Troccoli, though she never books her own concerts, to call Lori.

God seemed to soften hearts toward Sandi Patty, though she had fallen, showing His desire for believers to pass on a heritage of grace.

God seemed to hone the message of Heritage Keepers, reminding us all of His call, of His desire for women to embrace their holy heritage, and to tell the next generation.

I have had the sense that each believer has been called by God to carry the same message. Continually I have said to Lori: "Lori, this is bigger than you. This is bigger than me. This is bigger than Heritage Keepers."

"I know, Dee," she says, shaking her head in amazement. "I know."

If you are familiar with Aslan, the lion of C.S. Lewis' *The Lion, the Witch, and the Wardrobe,* who represents Jesus, you will understand the phrase: "Aslan is on the move." Again and again as I have been a part of Heritage Keepers, as I have written this book and talked to the people touched by Heritage Keepers, I have often felt the warm breath of the Lion of Judah on my neck. Many times I have sensed Aslan on the move, as when I wrote the difficult chapter concerning Sandi Patty and sensed God's anointing so strongly. When I sent it to her, her first reaction was pain. *I don't want to be a part of this book,* she thought. *But if I am, couldn't Dee just talk around the issue?* But Sandi submitted herself to God, shared the chapter with her accountability group, and talked to her pastor. Four days later when we talked, she said:

> *God put in my heart: "Sandi, I am the God of truth and where there is truth, I am there. So trust Me." With the woman caught in adultery, Jesus extended her grace, but He didn't gloss over her sin. Maybe for too long the church has tried to gloss it over and call it by a different name. I think that when we can begin to get real, God can do a deeper work. So, Dee, that's where I am.*

I wept—at Sandi's honesty, at a God who would bend down and speak to her, and for my own sin. For when a sister honestly confesses her own sin, the pure light of God burns in our own hearts and reveals the dark places we have hidden, which we have tried to "talk around." And that is the beginning of revival.

In *My Daughter, My Daughter* you will see what happens when we stop avoiding God, but instead turn and run to Him, no matter how painful that may initially seem. I have seen a transformation in Sandi as she has continually chosen, over the past few years, to run toward God. After she chose, for example, to allow me to share what I have in chapter 10 of this book, I have seen Sandi's ministry with Heritage Keepers deepen. Just before this book went to print, something happened I will never, ever, forget.

At the close of the Heritage Keepers Conference in Indianapolis in the summer of '99, Carol Kent was giving an altar call, asking women to come forward and meet with various speakers for prayer, including prayer for salvation, recommitment, depression, and prodigal children. Sandi whispered something to Lori, and Lori nodded. Then Sandi came up behind Carol, tapped her on the shoulder, and whispered to her. Taking the mike, Sandi said, "I know this wasn't planned—but I'd like to pray with women who have been in an affair or are in an affair right now." Sandi then walked down the steps, and women began to make their way up the aisles to her. When it was time for the closing song, which Sandi was supposed to sing, the mike was handed down to her. She began singing, "You Have Set Me Free." She stayed down below, at first, and sang to each of the eight weeping women who had prayed with her, looking into their eyes, one by one. Then she climbed the steps to the stage and sang to all of us, and a holy presence filled the arena. It was a beautiful picture of a woman who, because she did not flee from her holy heritage, had been set free, and now was leading others into that freedom as well. I thought: *God, You are so good. You told Sandi that her submission to You would take her into a deeper walk with You, and here it is, the fulfillment of your promise.*

And He will do the same for you.

Revival often begins with pain, in the hearts of individuals or in the hearts of a nation. But when that pain causes us to seek the Lord with our whole heart and respond as He would have us respond, our pain is replaced with an incredible peace, and a spirit that is revived to the goodness and power of God.

THE SIGNS OF REVIVAL

What are the historical signs of revival?
Prayer and fasting
A return to the Word

Genuine repentance
Hearts restored to a first love for Jesus
Reconciliation between believers
Many saved

With Promise Keepers, all these signs were present. This men's movement was so big and loud it caught even the attention of the secular media, which is typically myopic to genuine Christianity. Though the media missed the quiet prayer movements behind the scenes, it's hard to miss millions of men filling up football stadiums, raising robust voices in praise, weeping, and embracing their brothers of different denominations and colors. Something was happening. Surely the women who welcomed their changed men home suspected God was on the move.

The movement for the women has been quieter and more diverse, but as I have crisscrossed this country giving seminars and talking to women whose lives have been changed through in-depth Bible studies or conferences, I am aware that God is bending down and calling His daughters as well, for I have repeatedly heard *one message*. When the *same message* comes to many individual women who are earnestly seeking God, you begin to suspect that God, indeed, may be the One calling.

What intrigues me about Heritage Keepers is its message, for it is the same message God has been communicating from various sources at the close of the twentieth century.

Gwen Shamblin's Weigh Down Workshop has discovered a parallel between the way God worked in lives of the Israelites and how He works in our lives today. The hidden things she has uncovered have resulted in revitalized lives. Gwen has often said, "This message is bigger than me. It is bigger than Weigh Down." Participants in Weigh Down have a contagious excitement, and so they are telling the next generation.

Beth Moore's *A Woman's Heart: God's Dwelling Place* has discovered a parallel between the way God worked in the lives of the Israelites and how He works in our lives today. The hidden things she has uncovered have resulted in revitalized lives. When I see Beth's enthusiasm in her opening video, her excitement in sharing this message, I understand. This message is bigger than Beth. It is bigger than her ministry. Participants are excited and long to pass what they have discovered to the next generation.

Henry Blackaby and Claude King's *Experiencing God* has discovered a parallel between the way God worked in the lives of the Israelites and how He works in our lives today. The hidden things they uncovered have resulted in revitalized lives. So many people have told me, with excitement, that they decided to change careers or ministries because of the hidden things they found in this study. Their enthusiasm is spreading down to the next generation.

As Heritage Keepers began to take shape, God impressed Psalm 78 on our hearts as the backbone of this ministry. This psalm looks back at the way God worked in the lives of the Israelites and urges us to learn from their story. He says he has "hidden things" which will emerge as we study the story. He wants us to learn these things so that the next generation will know.

If I were to sum up the message I am seeing repeated in all of the above movements, I would say God longs for us to look back at our holy heritage, discover the hidden things, and remember them today! But it is stronger than that. We must be:

Against forgetting our holy heritage

God is grieved when His people forget the stories of old or are too lazy to look beneath the surface, for though embracing the literal story is part of our treasure, it isn't the whole treasure—there is more, and we must pan for it, like nuggets of gold. Every book in the Old Testament contains a hidden picture, a parable. In the miracles in Exodus we see not only the power of God, but if we look deeper, we see a parable. Just as God's people were in literal slavery, we were (or are) in slavery to sin. Just as God's people needed a deliverer (Moses), we need a deliverer (Jesus). Just as God's people needed to remember what God had done in the past so they could hope in Him in the present, so must we. We must feast on the Word and its meat, and allow it to change our lives. We must value this holy heritage more than our grandmother's bone china, for *this* is the inheritance God longs for us to pass down to our children. We must be:

Against forgetting our holy heritage

We are weak, we easily forget, like our ancestors. Though God parted the sea for them, they murmured against Him in the desert, saying,

But can he also give us food? (Psalm 78:20b)

God is calling to us, pleading with us to remember His mighty acts, our holy heritage. Since you have picked up this book and begun to read, I believe He is calling to you as well:

My daughter, my precious child,
incline your ear, and I will teach you
hidden things from your holy heritage....

Whether or not you grew up in a home that loved Jesus, you *do* have a holy heritage. If you have placed your trust in Christ, you are a child of Abraham, a daughter of Sarah. Therefore, even if you did not have godly grandparents or godly parents, you still have ancestors who walked with God. God wants you to remember these ancestors: Abraham, Sarah, and more—so that you can then pass on this holy heritage.

GOD INVITES US TO JOIN HIM IN HIS PLANS

Bob and Lori Beckler of Heritage Keepers, along with thousands of Christians, have been impacted by *Experiencing God*. Blackaby and King have looked back at our holy heritage to discover how God worked with the Israelites. They noticed a pattern. Repeatedly, *God* came up with a plan and then would invite His servants, one by one, to join Him.

When God heard the groaning of the Israelites in slavery, He had a plan to deliver them and He invited Moses to join Him. Moses didn't come up with the plan; he discovered God's plan and joined Him.

Bob and Lori wondered if that, indeed, might be happening to them. Surely God had been at work with Promise Keepers. They wondered: *Was He now inviting them to join Him in a new wave to impact the hearts of women?*

It is my conviction that God did speak to Lori and Bob in His still small voice. He showed them, not the whole plan at once, but a step at a time, the way He did with Moses. I am persuaded that this dream of calling women to embrace their heritage is not Lori and Bob's dream, but God's dream, and He simply invited them to join Him. His desire to have His children embrace their heritage and pass it on is not new—but He seems to be repeating it today to His children, bending down and calling them, like the Pied Piper He can be, to join Him. In the particular venture of Heritage Keepers, He has invited married women and single women. He has invited women who have a wonderful heritage such as Point of Grace, Carol Kent, and Billy Graham's youngest daughter, Ruth McIntyre (Bunny, but she doesn't want to be called Bunny anymore!). He has also called those who may be the first link in the chain, like Kathy Troccoli.

During the closing hour of a recent Heritage Keepers conference when the speakers and singers sat on sofas in a cozy setting on stage, speaker RoseAnne Coleman quipped: "When God talks to me, He calls me 'Baby,' because God is from the South—He just works everywhere else too."

Kathy Troccoli, who is from New York, said, "To me, He says, 'Yo! Are you talkin' to me?'"

We roared, and yet, the truth is, He does call, He does speak, and His call is very personal. He knows us, He knit us together in our mother's womb, and He knows how to speak to each of us personally.

GOD IS MINDFUL OF YOU

The thought that the God who made the universe is mindful of us overwhelms me every day of my life. I identify with the shepherd David who looked up at the starry night, the canopy of constellations, and wondered:

When I consider your heavens,
the work of your fingers,
the moon and the stars,
which you have set in place,
what is man that you are **mindful** *of him?* (Psalm 8:3-4)

The Old Testament is filled with stories of God bending down and guiding His children with His mighty hand: parting the Red Sea, guiding with a pillar of light by day and a pillar of fire by night, and feeding His children with manna falling gently from the sky.

Likewise in the New Testament, angels lit up the sky that first Christmas to let man know that God, indeed, was mindful of him. Mary, the mother of Jesus, was overwhelmed with emotion when she realized God had bent down and called her, specifically, to join Him in His amazing plan to bring His Son to earth. In her Magnificat she says:

My soul glorifies the Lord
and my spirit rejoices in God my Savior,
for he has been **mindful**
of the humble state of his servant. (Luke 1:46-48)

Does that same God still bend down? Is He still mindful of us? Does He still call us to join Him in His plans?

Some think it presumptuous to say God is speaking to us. Why would a holy God be interested in us? Though it is amazing, the evidence is strong that He is. However, some have tarnished this golden truth by attributing "the leading of the Lord" to their own selfish desires. In order to justify themselves in their own eyes or in the eyes of others, they say God led them when, in fact, they simply wanted a new house or a new husband. I liked what Robert Duvall said in the movie *The Apostle* when his wife, played by Farrah Fawcett, told him God had told her to leave him and to have an affair with the youth pastor.

"**Our** God told you that?"

God never leads against His Word, but He does lead. In fact, He tells us, in Psalm 78, to *remember* how He led His children of old, and to tell these historical stories to our children so they too might trust in Him and seek His face. He still bends down and whispers to His children. He still guides. He is still mindful of us.

GOD LONGS TO SPEAK TO YOU—HE EVEN KNOWS YOUR NAME

God speaks to me daily through His Word and the nudge of His Spirit. But has He ever spoken my name? Yes. Not often, but He has.

The first time God called my name was when I was a very new Christian and a relatively new mommy, the mother of a three year old and a new baby. My husband, a medical intern, was gone every third night. Those nights I paced the floor, sleepless, as I was convinced someone was going to break into the house and murder me and our precious boys. We lived in a rented house on Seattle's Puget Sound. (Yes, I was sleepless in Seattle.) I imagined a madman rowing his boat stealthily to the edge of our yard, pulling a nylon grotesquely over his head, stealing behind the magnolia bushes in the black of the night, shattering the glass of my ground floor bedroom window, and leaping upon me in my bed with a knife. I had definitely given way to hysterical fears! (True daughters of Sarah, as you will discover in this book, don't give way to hysterical fears.)

At a Bible study for young moms, an older woman (she was probably thirty) saw my bleary eyes and asked me if our new baby was keeping me up. When I told her it was my fears that were keeping me up, she counseled me to pray through Psalm 34 before I went to bed. I had done that, but here I was still awake, and it was two in the morning. I was seated on the steps leading to the upstairs, sobbing into my open Bible. I had just read Psalm 34:7, which says:

The angel of the Lord encamps around those who fear him.

And I thought, as I wept, *But what if it is God's will for me to die at the hands of a madman?*

And then, in the still of the night, He spoke—not audibly, but in my heart, so clearly, that it arrested me:

Dee

He had spoken my name. I held my breath and listened:

You are going to die. But not that way.

Now He really had my attention. I wanted to know more. I asked, "*How* am I going to die?"

Now God was silent. He wasn't going to answer that question. He had told me all I needed to know. I was going to die. But not that way. I could stop my hysteria.

I went to bed and slept peacefully. Never again have I lost sleep for fear of being murdered by a madman. Like a father to a daughter, He reached out to me and calmed my fears. The other two times I remember God saying my name were, again, when I was anxious, overcome by fear. Intriguingly, that is also a pattern I see in Scripture. Like a daddy who rushes in to stop the nightmare of his precious little girl, lifting her from her bed and soothing her in his strong arms, God comes to us in our need. Sometimes, He tenderly calls us *Daughter*:

Then the woman, seeing that she could not go unnoticed, came trembling and fell at his feet. . . . Then he said to her, "Daughter, your faith has healed you. Go in peace." (Luke 8:47-48)

Sometimes, He even speaks our name.

What is the matter, Hagar? He spoke to a single mother who had been cast out of her home. She was sobbing. And then. God spoke her name, through an angel, and assured her of His care and provision. (Genesis 21:8-21)

Martha, Martha, you are worried and upset about many things, but only one thing is needed. She had worked herself into a sweat fixing an elaborate meal for Jesus, but more stressful than her physical strain were the turbulent emotions churning inside her: anxiety, irritation, and anger—growing by the moment as she watched her younger sister sitting at the feet of Jesus, not lifting a finger to help. Jesus rebuked her, but so tenderly—He said her name twice, a sign of endearment. (Luke 10:38-42)

Mary. Just her name, that was all that was needed for her to recognize Him. She thought He was dead, the One who meant everything to her, who had delivered her from the prison of seven demons. Sobbing, she cried out to the man she thought was the gardener, pleading for his help in finding the body of Jesus. And then. He spoke her name. In that instant she turned and recognized her Savior and Lord. (John 20:15-18)

The same intimate relationship He had with the holy women of old He is still having with women today. He longs to guide you, to comfort you, to whisper to you. In the next chapter you will read how God whispered to Lori Beckler, calling her to change from booking conferences for the world to booking conferences for Him. But before you read it, do the Bible study, for the primary way He will bend down and speak to you is during those moments when you curl up with Him and His Word.

Also, and we will look at this truth more deeply in the next chapter, God doesn't just scatter His precious gold about—He has protected it by hiding it in parables, in riddles from the past. You have a heritage of pure gold—but you must pan for it. I would encourage you to pan on your own, but then to get together with a small group of sisters in Christ to share your discoveries. Psalm 78 tells us that these stories contain *hidden truths.* The advantage of meeting in a small group is that you will have your sisters in Christ to help you discern the difference between fool's gold and real gold and to do something with the amazing nuggets God gives you. If you *are* doing this in a small group, please read the short section in the back of the book, in Appendix A, for making your group the best and most nurturing it can be.

As you delve into the Word, you will undoubtedly experience attacks from the Enemy, for Satan fears the powerful Word of God. He will try to discourage you from meeting with God. When you sit down with your Bible, he may whisper: *Just put a load of wash in*. If you are undiscerning, you hop up, put a load of wash in, and then he says: *You were going to call your mom*. Pretty soon he has successfully distracted you and somehow—you don't get back to God's powerful Word. You need to recognize the Enemy and shut your ears to him. I am convinced he stalks us, as women, because we are the relational sex. He knows that if he can lead us astray, as he did Eve, we may lead those close to us astray as well. He targeted Lori, as you will see later in the story. It is through the Word of God, the sword of the Spirit, that you can defeat the Enemy. You will find the following study divided into three quiet times (each new day is marked with a sunrise).

God is calling to you, saying:

My daughter, My daughter
My precious child,
Incline your ear and I will
teach you hidden things. . . .

Panning for Heritage Gold

Please read the hints in Appendix A (p. 256) for making your study and discussion time richer.

☀ Get-Acquainted Opener for Small Groups: Share your name, a little about yourself, and, in one breath, one time when you sensed God was mindful of you.

1. What stood out to you from the text and Scriptures in the first chapter? Why?

Read Psalm 8.

2. What thought amazes the psalmist in verse 3? Does this thought amaze you? Explain.

☼ 3. Meditate on the following situations when God spoke an individual's name and write down everything you discover.

A. Genesis 15:1-6

B. Genesis 21:17-21

C. 1 Samuel 3

D. Luke 1:13

E. Luke 1:30-31

4. Did you see any similarities in the above? What does that teach you about God?

5. When God repeats a name, it is often from loving concern and a sign of endearing tenderness. How do you see this in each of the following?

    A. Luke 22:31-32

    B. Matthew 23:37

    C. Luke 10:38-42

6. Pan for gold in Luke 10:38-42 by reflecting on the following:

    A. Look carefully at the pronouns in verse 38 and find evidence that the disciples may have stayed elsewhere in Bethany and that Jesus came alone to Martha's home.

    B. What evidence do you find of Martha's hospitality in verse 38?

    C. Find three things about Mary in verse 39.

    D. How is Martha described in verse 40a?

E. In verse 40, how does Martha accuse Jesus? How does she accuse Mary?

F. How do you see the tenderness of Jesus toward Martha in verse 41? Why do you think He is concerned for her?

G. How do you see the tenderness of Jesus toward Mary in verse 42? Why do you think He is concerned for her?

7. What do you think is more valuable in God's eyes: worship or service?

8. Learning how to spend time with the Lord, sitting at His feet, listening, and worshiping, is vital. Those who have succeeded in developing this habit often choose the same time of day, the same place, and have a particular plan of study. How might you follow in their steps?

☼ Read John 11 as an overview.

9. Describe what happened. What are some of the main lessons you believe God would want you to understand from this story?

Note, in particular, Mary. What similarities do you see in her that you discovered in Luke 10?

Read John 12:1-11.

10. Describe what happened.

11. Pan for gold in the above.

    A. Why do you think the facts mentioned in verse 1 are significant?

    B. Describe the beauty of Mary's worship. Find everything you can in verse 3.

    C. Once again Jesus defends Mary. How?

D. Though He had told them, His disciples still didn't understand He was going to die. What evidence do you find that Mary *did* understand?

E. From this incident, what do you think the Lord values more: worship or service? Why?

12. Mary of Bethany exemplifies a daughter who listened. How does Jesus say she will be blessed in Matthew 26:13?

13. The heart of Heritage Keepers is Psalm 78. Read just the opening verse. How do you see tenderness? What is the opening plea?

PRAYER TIME:

Stand in a circle holding hands. Pray a simple blessing for the woman on your right such as, "Thank You Lord for Sally and her cheerful spirit" or "Help Linda to feel welcome at this, her first Bible study." (If you are shy, pray silently and squeeze the hand of the woman on your left so she will know it is her turn to pray.)

I Will Show You Hidden Things

God does, indeed, speak to us, and I will show you how He called to Lori in a moment. But it is important to understand that our God is mysterious, and when He reveals a plan, it is often one step at a time, rather than the whole itinerary. Also, when He speaks in His Word, sometimes it is in parables and riddles. In Psalm 78 He tells His children He has *hidden things* that He will only share with some. Why?

HIDDEN THINGS

Do you remember when Jesus said, "Don't throw your pearls before swine?" (Matthew 7:6) I have a beautiful diamond ring that belonged to my mother. I'm not going to let my three-year-old granddaughter play with it. But I might give it to her when she is a woman with the maturity to appreciate and take care of it. Parables are like that. They protect God's jewels until the person can appreciate them and use them as intended. The great truths of God are too precious to be left open and unattended for anyone who happens by.

God speaks in parables to protect His treasure. He reveals His heart, His hidden truths, only to those who seek and obey. The rest, even His children, squander their lives like the Children of Israel, who wandered for forty long years in the wilderness.

The common thread I have observed as I consider the Bible studies and conferences bringing revival to women is a call to remember our holy heritage and to *discover* the hidden truths in that heritage. It excites me to see, for example:

Kay Arthur (founder of Precept Ministries) helping women to understand the hidden precepts in God's Word. Kay directs us to buy colored markers so that we can mark our Bibles with different colors and symbols as we discover the *hidden things* from our holy heritage.

Anne Graham Lotz (second child of Billy and Ruth Graham, and acclaimed Bible teacher) helping women to discover both the literal and spiritual message in various passages. In her book *The Vision of His Glory*, on the Book of Revelation, she helps readers find the literal facts and then interpret their deeper hidden meaning.

Beth Moore (author of *A Woman's Heart: God's Dwelling Place*) helping women understand the symbolism of the tabernacle in our holy heritage, and how these hidden pictures can help us to understand who God is and how much He loves us and wants us to walk in holiness. Women are mesmerized as Beth unveils one *hidden picture* after another in her video series.

Gwen Shamblin (founder of Weigh Down) successfully helping thousands to understand they have been in slavery, as were the Israelites in Egypt, and that they must leave Egypt and the false god of food and go through the desert of testing to the Promised Land of freedom. Even though it makes me smile to see Gwen dressed up in a robe and teaching in the desert with the pyramids in the background, I see how powerfully God is using her to reveal *hidden things* from our holy heritage.

The Beckler and Bowling families (Heritage Keepers) helping women reclaim their holy heritage by reflecting on Psalm 78, that

God revealed through their grandmother's Bible, to be the backbone of Heritage Keepers. It is in this psalm that God calls, saying, "I will utter *hidden things,* things from of old...." (Psalm 78:2)

Many women have tasted and seen that the Lord is good, and many women's conferences in addition to Heritage Keepers have whetted women's appetites. Many women are placing their faith in Christ for the first time and others are experiencing a growing hunger for the meat of the Word, for Bible studies into which they can sink their teeth. They've grown past milk and they don't want cotton candy—material that Kathy Troccoli calls "Christianity lite" because it leaves no lasting impact on the heart or mind. They want the Word! God seems to be calling His daughters to look back at their holy heritage and discover the truths from their scriptural past that can equip them to live holy lives.

Charles Spurgeon, the nineteenth-century preacher, whom I quoted in the opening of this chapter, explains why we must seek for the most wondrous part of God's work, His hidden wisdom:

> *Those who do not look below the surface miss the best part of what he would teach us. The devout naturalist ransacks nature, the earnest student of history pries into hidden facts and dark stories, and the man of God digs into the mines of Scripture, and hoards up each grain of its golden truth.* [2]

Spurgeon says that the reason the Israelites forgot the mighty miracles of God was that they didn't really understand the hidden pictures, explaining:

> *What is not understood will soon be forgotten. Men feel little interest in preserving husks; if they know nothing of the inner kernel they will take no care of the shells.* [3]

Likewise today, Christians may know facts, but fail to understand the hidden pictures. I am continually amazed at the depth of the Word of God. I have, for example, spoken on the Book of Ruth for fifteen years. I thought, *I know this book. I can practically recite it by memory! I'm ready to write a study guide on Ruth.* Yet when I began to do some fresh research in order to write *A Woman's Journey Through Ruth,* **more** pictures came into view. I was fascinated to discover how the land paralleled the spiritual state of the people's hearts, from "a famine in the land" in the opening to a "plentiful harvest" at the close. I also saw, for the first time, the repeated picture of Ruth filling up Naomi's empty arms, and of how we are to fill up one another's empty arms. Those lovely pictures were there all along, but I had not seen them. I was as excited as our daughter Beth was when she was first fitted with glasses at the age of twelve. (Beth, who grew up in an orphanage, could not see faces or even the huge E at the top of the eye chart.) As we walked outside the optometrist's office she stopped, frozen on the sidewalk. "Ohhh," she gasped as she saw trees, flowers, and her mother's face clearly for the first time.

This book will uncover hidden pictures from your holy heritage, lacing them together with the exciting story of Heritage Keepers, to help you understand. In an amazing way, hidden truths from your holy ancestors paralleled the evolving story of the people who were called to Heritage Keepers. Here is a glimpse of what is to come to whet your appetite:

Satan targeted Eve. Do you understand we are all daughters of Eve and that Satan targets women?
Light will be shed when you see why he targeted Lori, the founder of Heritage Keepers. This wisdom will help protect you.

Peter tells us to be daughters of Sarah. Do you understand what that means?
Light will be shed when you read how the Beckler and Bowling women walked by faith and did not give way to hysterical fears in order to found Heritage Keepers.

God was pleased with the Hebrew midwives. Do you understand why and how we might follow their model?

Light will be shed when you read the Kathy Troccoli story. God is using her to minister to victims of abortion and to save lives with her heartrending song "A Baby's Prayer."

Miriam forgot her holy heritage and fell into sin. God never fully restored her. Why does God restore some fallen leaders and not others?
Light will be shed when you read the Sandi Patty story. God wants you to honestly confess your sin so that you can have a deeper walk with Him.

When we understand, then we are equipped to pass on this heritage to the next generation—not the empty husks, but the hidden golden corn. This is the message God seems to be whispering, not only to the founders of Heritage Keepers, but to His daughters everywhere. When God whispers the same thing to different people, we can at least begin to consider that it is God, and not we ourselves, who is leading. Come with me to December of 1995, when Lori Beckler first had the sense that God might be calling her to change from booking conferences for the world to booking conferences for Him: conferences called Heritage Keepers.

GOD WHISPERS: WICHITA, KANSAS, DECEMBER 1995

Lori was working for a travel convention business: planning meetings in cities, booking the hotels, the convention facilities, and arranging all the details. This, along with mothering two preteens and preparing for Christmas, filled her days to the brim. Yet, on a December afternoon as she was seated at her office computer, suddenly, there was a thought.

What about a women's style Promise Keepers?

Lori said, "It wasn't an audible voice—just a thought that seemed to come out of thin air. I had so much to do that day, I tried to concentrate. I returned to my task, but the thought wouldn't go away. Every time I tried to concentrate on the task at hand, this thought came back."

What about a women's style Promise Keepers?

"Pretty soon I was excited, yet at the same time, I was telling myself, *You don't need one more thing to do.*"

After work that evening, Lori took their children, Nicole and Daniel, to a the final game in the playoffs for the high school basketball team that her husband, Bob, was coaching.

This was a huge night for Trinity Academy and the pregame conversation in the bleachers centered on the game. But Lori's mind was distracted. She had a growing conviction that God was calling:

You, Lori. You and Bob. I'm calling you to begin a women's style Promise Keepers.

Before the game began, Lori walked around the floor sharing this thought with friends and family. Each listened intently, but they knew Lori. She's a visionary (some would say "dreamer"), and visionaries can get ahead of God. Each one told her to pray, to see if God confirmed it in other ways. Lori hadn't talked to Bob yet, and since the game was about to begin, she found a seat in the bleachers. But then she caught sight of her husband. He was standing alone, watching the door from which the players would soon run. Though she knew that the moment before the game began might not be the best time to interrupt the coach, she couldn't contain her excitement. She hopped down from the bleachers to Bob's side, the story tumbling out. She closed with:

Bob—I really think God might be calling us to do this women's conference.

THE SAME SPIRIT WILL SAY THE SAME THING

When our sons, who love sports, heard this story, they were appalled. Our son-in-law, Jeremie, said, "Didn't Lori realize how *terrible* her timing was?"

What amazes *me* is Bob's reaction. I asked him, "Weren't you irritated that Lori chose this, of all moments, to talk to you?"

Bob smiled, shaking his head. "Well, I did think, *Lori, you should know better than to come to me at a time like this.* Yet there was a look in her eyes—a look I'd never seen her have before, but a look that I was going to see again and again during our faith journey. It arrested me, stopped my irritation, and caused me to listen long enough to hear the overwhelming thought that had seized her heart. But then the players were running out on the floor and I said, "Okay, Lori—we'll talk about it later."

The game was thrilling, each team gaining the lead for just minutes and then losing it. In the final moments the gym was filled with electricity. "What happened next," Lori told me, her green eyes dancing, "was so ironic. This was the semi-final game in overtime and Bob was sooooo focused as the coach. With less than a minute to go he was screaming instructions to a player." Lori laughed. "Do you know how you remember scenes that were pivotal in your life? Bob remembers the kid, his number, and his expression as if it were a frame in a movie, frozen. The opponents had changed their defense. Bob yelled to Matt Kutilek, number 20, *not* to run the play they had originally planned. Matt looked back at Bob with a shocked look, and then, at that very crucial moment, Bob heard a still small voice, bringing back my voice:

Bob—I really think God might be calling us to do this women's conference.

Lori clasped her hands behind her head and leaned back reflectively. "I think God used that moment, of all moments, to get Bob's attention—because a women's conference is the last thing Bob would be thinking about during that moment. The logical thing for him to be thinking about was *Is Matt Kutilek, this kid who is learning about obedience and life, going to obey me—or is he going to throw the game?* Instead, Bob is hearing: *Bob—I really think God might be calling us to do this women's conference.*

When Bob reflected on that scene, he said: "Having Lori's words flash back into my mind at that crucial moment startled me. Though I focused again on the game (and Matt obeyed and Trinity won the game), it was a different kind of focus, because I knew God was starting to do something. Lori and I had to talk." Bob paused and then spoke with conviction: "God came to Lori and to me, to each of us, in our own arenas: to Lori He spoke in the midst of her convention business, and to me, in the midst of athletics." Intriguingly, God interrupted each of them, perhaps so they would know the voice was His and not their own.

THE MOST EXCITING LIFE POSSIBLE

I love the way the Apostle John opens his first letter, with breathless excitement at having "seen with his eyes, looked at, and touched, 'the Word of life." Then he eagerly invites his readers into fellowship with Jesus and His children. When two (or more) people are connected to Jesus, they have a fellowship unlike any fellowship—because the Holy Spirit can whisper the same thing to each of them. When I spoke during Heritage Keepers in 1998 to twelve thousand women at their return engagement to Market Square Arena, home of the Indiana Pacers, I said:

> I have a son who lives here in Indianapolis who tells me how exciting it is to watch your wonderful Pacers (women cheer) play basketball in this arena.

> But as exciting as the fellowship of basketball players is, our fellowship is much more exciting—because our fellowship is with the Father, and with His Son, Jesus Christ (women cheer so loudly that the secular media picked up this soundbite for the six o'clock news).

How can anything, really, compare to the fellowship we have together because of knowing Jesus? When we know Jesus, the Holy Spirit dwells within us and can whisper *the same thing* to each of us.

Heather, Denise, Shelley, and Terry, the singers of Point of Grace, whose first large women's conference was Heritage Keepers, have experienced this very thing. One of the rules they have for choosing songs for their albums (or even what they wear on stage) is that they each seek God's face individually and then come together. They are convinced that if they are each seeking God then His Spirit can tell each of them the same thing. If they are not unanimous on a song it does not go into an album.

This leads me into the first *hidden thing* from your heritage that I have discovered and am so excited to share with you. I believe it can protect you from fruitless wilderness wanderings and help you discover the true voice of God.

A HIDDEN TRUTH FROM YOUR HOLY HERITAGE

It's clear, and not hidden, that we were never intended to walk this pilgrimage alone—we need each other in the body of Christ! We need the encouragement and the accountability. Kathy Troccoli, for example, has three accountability partners, three women who refresh and revive her with their wit, wisdom, and the warmth of open hearts and homes. (You'll meet them later.) God tells us clearly to meet together to encourage one another (Hebrews 10:25), and you will gain even more from this book if you study and discuss it with a small group sisters in Christ.

What is not so apparent immediately, but a truth that more and more believers are realizing is that *one of the most reliable ways to hear God is to each listen to Him individually and then come together to see if He has spoken the same thing to each of you.* Sometimes there will be complete unity, other times it may not be unanimous but there will be a sweet spirit of submission that says, "I don't see it yet, but since the rest of you do and since I know you are earnestly seeking God's face, I will support you."

As I have been privileged to work briefly with hundreds of women's ministries, I have seen the most fruit in those who have grasped *this* truth. There are ministries that have done things the same way forever, and they are asking God to bless them. They are no longer seeking God. Instead of continuing up the mountain, they are circling at the same level. Then there are groups that continually seek God's face, open to His counsel, to see if He has a fresh new path to take them higher. Often He hones the original plan, as I have seen Him hone the plan for Heritage Keepers.

At first it just seemed God was calling the Becklers to do a women's conference, not unlike many of the women's conferences available today, but as they continued to listen, He became more specific. He was calling them to help women embrace their holy heritage and pass it to the next generation. Likewise, women's ministries that keep seeking God keep moving higher up the mountain, following in His steps. They continue to pray in earnest, they come together, and they move out when God whispers the same thing to each of them. They look for where God is at work, they listen, and they pray for like-mindedness as a confirming sign. The God of our ancestors is still alive, still whispers, and still confirms His message by repeating the same thing to those who seek His face.

I have often told the joke that the reason the Israelites wandered for forty years was because the men were unwilling to stop and ask for directions. Yet there is truth in that jest, though it was *both* the men and the women who were unwilling to listen to God. They did not seek His face. They did not listen. So they could not obey. They turned to idols for help rather than the living God. So what should have been a two-week trip took forty years, and most never made it, for the Scripture says:

God was not pleased with most of them; their bodies were scattered over the desert. (1 Corinthians 10:5)

God longs for us to look at our holy heritage and learn from these stories—both the positive and negative models:

These things happened to them as examples and were written down as warnings for us, on whom the fulfillment of the ages has come. (1 Corinthians 10:11)

We need to seek God and turn from our own ways, and from idols. When we wake up we need to run into His arms. When we are in pain we need to run to Him, not to the mall or a pan of brownies. And if we are unsure if we are hearing His voice, one of the best things we can do is to seek His face with another believer. That is the beauty of the body of Christ.

Likewise, one of the blessings of a Christian marriage is that a husband and wife can be a check and a balance for one another by seeing if God gives the same idea to each of them. As you study one of the first couples in our holy heritage your understanding of what made their marriage so unusual will help you to remember their story, and to pass on a golden principle to the next generation.

ABRAHAM AND SARAH: COHEIRS

The ancient historian Josephus says that Abraham was remarkable in breaking away from the gods of his fathers, setting out from Haran in obedience to the voice of just one God, the God who often refers to Himself as the God of Abraham, Isaac, and Jacob. Sarah sojourned with him, supporting him not only in this dramatic move of faith, but in many others. Yet even Abraham and Sarah were mortals, and like all mortals, they had feet of clay. The times when Abraham and Sarah got into trouble and brought enormous pain into their lives were when they failed to *each* seek God individually. One would get an idea, and because each loved and respected the other so much, sometimes the other would fail to act as a check and a balance.

For example, when they traveled into Egypt, Abraham had the bright idea of misleading the Pharaoh into thinking Sarah was just his sister. That way the Pharaoh could sleep with beautiful Sarah, which Abraham knew he would want to do, without killing Abraham! (You can read about this in Genesis 12—note how shocked the Egyptians were at Abraham's deception.) One of our responsibilities as "coheirs" is to act as a check and a balance by seeking God individually and encouraging our mate to walk by faith and not by sight. Instead of saying, "Okay, honey," Sarah should have asked these questions:

Is this glorifying to God?
Is this consistent with His Word?
Do I have a peace about this plan?

Likewise, there were times Sarah led Abraham astray as well. God had promised Sarah and Abraham they would have a child, but ten years passed and there was no child. Walter Wangerin, in *The Book of God*, renders the story:

> God had aroused the desire inside of Sarah, and it would not lie down and die again. Every night it plucked at her heart: *Where is it? Where is the child of my own womb?*

> No, Sarah could never again be content with her fate—not after laughter and dancing and trust and all the changes the promise had caused in her life.

> Therefore, she took matters into her own hands.

> … "Abraham?" she said. "I have an idea."[4]

Sarah asked Abraham to sleep with her maidservant Hagar to conceive a child who would become Abraham and Sarah's heir. Instead of saying, "Okay, honey," Abraham should have asked:

Is this glorifying to God?

Is this consistent with His Word?

Do I have a peace about this plan?

Perhaps if Abraham had sought God's face individually he would have vetoed Sarah's idea, but instead, he followed Sarah's suggestion, slept with Hagar, and conceived Ishmael. God was *not* leading. Stepping out of God's path led to tremendous heartache for them: for Hagar, for Ishmael, and for all the Israelites and Arabs in generations to come.

No wonder years later, when Sarah comes to Abraham with another bold plan he hesitates. By this time, Ishmael is a teenager and Sarah and Abraham have been given the promised biological son: Isaac. Ishmael is mocking Isaac and Sarah wants Ishmael and his mother, Hagar, out of their lives. "Send them away," she tells Abraham.

Abraham is tremendously grieved, for he loves his son Ishmael dearly, and, no doubt, remembers that the last time he did as Sarah requested it had been an enormous mistake. This time, Abraham seeks God. If God is leading Sarah, then God can tell Abraham the same thing. This is what God tells him:

> *Do not be so distressed about the boy and your maidservant. Listen to whatever Sarah tells you, because it is through Isaac that your offspring will be reckoned. I will make the son of the maidservant into a nation also, because he is your offspring.* (Genesis 21:12-13)

Abraham is remembered for his faith and obedience. It is easy to obey when God bends down and whispers something exciting; it's quite another thing when we don't like the agenda. Many believers do not truly obey God; it is just that at times they agree with Him, so they appear to obey. (C.S. Lewis said he had a dog like that!)

How do we know if our faith and obedience is genuine? When we obey the hard things, the whispers that differ from our own desires. Overall, Abraham was a mighty man of faith who obeyed the hard things. The grief that he felt in obeying God and sending Hagar and Ishmael away was enormous, but Abraham's faith carried him to obedience. God blessed that faith mightily, bringing peace to Abraham's nuclear family, yet also caring for Hagar and Ishmael.

GOD SPEAKS THROUGH HIS SPIRIT

When our daughter Sally was four I perched her on the kitchen counter after church to keep me company while I prepared Sunday dinner. "What did you learn in Sunday School today, honey?"

Sally scrunched her little forehead and answered, intently: "That God speaks in a still small voice."

I stopped dicing the cucumber for the salad—my knife in midair, astounded that our four year old had understood such an abstract concept. Perhaps we were raising a spiritual giant! Then she burst my bubble.

"That's why I can't hear Him," she stated, matter-of-factly, her legs swinging.

I laughed, and we have told this story many times, for the whole idea of God bending down and whispering to us can seem so wild—and yet, the evidence is strong that He does.

The primary way God speaks to us is through His Word. Sometimes He speaks through the nudge of His Spirit, but we need to check those nudges against His Word—for His Spirit never leads against His Word.

By the time Sally was a teenager, she was recognizing the voice of the Lord, even though He *does* speak in a still small voice. During the movie *Forrest Gump*, which she attended with her brother and his girlfriend, one of the main characters began blaspheming Jesus. The people in the theater began to laugh. Sally said, "It was an evil laugh." Sally became intensely uncomfortable. Then she sensed the nudge of His Spirit.

Just go.

At first she argued. *Basically this is an okay movie—it's just this scene—and pretty soon it will be over.* But then she sensed the nudge again.

Just go.

At that point, Sally was overcome with a fear of the Lord, sensing His holy presence. She leaned over to her brother and his girlfriend and said: "Let's just go."

J.R. and his girlfriend, Dianne, looked at each other, going through the same mental arguments Sally had just gone through. Then J.R. said, "You're right. Let's just go."

"As we walked out," Sally said, "an overwhelming sense of joy welled up in me. We had heard and obeyed God."

Are some believers more likely to hear God's still small voice than others? Yes.

As you study the holy men and women of old, you will find that those who obeyed were more likely to hear: Abraham, Sarah, Jochebed,

Moses. This makes sense—why would you keep speaking to someone who doesn't pay attention and obey?

GOD SPEAKS THROUGH HIS WORD

The most common way God speaks to us today is through His Word. I don't want to get ahead of the story, but suffice it for you to know that later, God revealed the name Heritage Keepers in a most amazing way through a highlighted Bible that belonged to Lori's grandmother. It is practically a "writing on the wall" story and the writing was Psalm 78.

God's first plea in Psalm 78 is to His people to listen—this is followed with a promise:

Oh my people, hear my teaching....
I will utter hidden things.

It is often in the hidden things that we discover the power to live a vibrant transformed life. Satan doesn't want us to discover these hidden things—so when we are getting close, he does his very best to distract us, to pull us off the path, by tempting us with lesser gods.

Satan was nearly successful with Lori. I'll tell you this fascinating story, but first, do the Bible study, so you don't miss the hidden gold.

Panning for Heritage Gold

☀ Get-Acquainted Opener for Small Groups: What are some reasons you might not simply *give* something of great value to another?

1. What stood out to you from the text and Scriptures in the second chapter? Why?

Read Psalm 78:1-4.

2. What promise does God give to those who will listen? (v. 2)

3. What does God want us to do with these hidden things? (v. 4)

Read Matthew 13:1-23.

4. What question do the disciples ask Jesus (v. 10) and how does He answer? (vv. 11-12)

5. Describe the prophesy from Isaiah that Jesus said was being fulfilled. (vv. 13-15)

Why did God hide truths from some and reveal them to others?

Why should we feel blessed if we see the hidden truths? (vv. 16-17)

6. What impact can understanding and obeying the hidden message of a parable or story have on your life? (v. 23)

☀ Read Genesis 15.

7. When God takes Abraham outside to consider the heavens, what promise does He give to him? (v. 5)

How does Abraham respond to God's words? (v. 6)

8. Often God gives us a story in the Old Testament with an important hidden meaning, and then clarifies the meaning through a caption in the New Testament. Read the caption in Romans 4:1-5. Put it in a sentence.

9. Abraham is the first man of faith in our holy heritage. To whom is Abraham a father according to Romans 4:16?

10. Another caption is given in Galatians 3:3-14. Who is blessed? (v. 9)

How are we not justified? (made right in the sight of God)

How did Christ make it possible for us to be justified? (v. 13)

How do we receive this justification? (v. 14)

☼ Though Abraham was a mighty man of faith, and his wife, Sarah, was a woman of faith, they each had lapses. We can learn a hidden truth from their lapses.

11. Describe Abraham's lapse of faith in Genesis 12:10-20 and again in Genesis 20. Describe the consequences as well.

Read Genesis 16.

12. Describe Sarah's lapse of faith here and the initial consequences. (v. 4)

13. Put yourself in Hagar's shoes. Describe all the emotions you think she might have had and why.

14. What evidence do you find that God knew Hagar and cared about her pain?

Does God promise Hagar relief from suffering? (v. 9) What does He tell her to do?

Read Genesis 21:1-20.

15. What do you learn about God from verses 1-7?

16. What irritated Sarah and how did she respond? (vv. 8-10)

17. How do you see God's compassion toward Abraham? (vv. 11-13)

18. What evidence do you see here that Abraham was truly walking by faith?

19. Where is God calling you to walk by faith and not by sight?

20. Describe Hagar's plight. Find everything you can by noticing the words and emotions. (vv. 14-16)

21. How do you see God's compassion toward Hagar and Ishmael? Find everything you can. (vv. 17-20)

In Genesis 16, Hagar's behavior led to their expulsion. Here it was Ishmael's behavior that led to expulsion. Yet, "on both occasions, God shows himself willing to rescue the afflicted even though their own behavior has provoked their persecution."[5]

22. What poor behavior on your part has brought grievous consequences?

23. God wants us to be "against forgetting." What gold have you discovered that has given you fresh understanding? (When we understand, it is less likely we will forget.) How will you apply it to your life?

PRAYER TIME:

Lift up your answer to question 19 or 23 in prayer and allow two or three of your sisters in Christ to support you in prayer. When there is a pause, another woman should do the same.

Three

*"Are you sure there are just four of you?" she asked.
"Two sons of Adam and two daughters of Eve, neither more
nor less?" and Edmund, with his mouth full of Turkish Delight,
kept on saying, "Yes, I told you that before."…
At last the Turkish Delight was all finished and Edmund
was looking very hard at the empty box.…
"Son of Adam, I should so much like to see your brother and
your two sisters. Will you bring them to me?"
"I'll try," said Edmund, still looking at the empty box.
"Because, if you did come again—bringing them with you of
course—I'd be able to give you some more Turkish Delight."[1]*

C.S. LEWIS,
THE LION, THE WITCH AND THE WARDROBE

A Snake in
the Grass

*W*hen I first read *The Lion, the Witch and the Wardrobe*, I wondered why Lewis kept referring to us as sons of Adam and daughters of Eve. Somehow, I didn't like that label. I wasn't sure I wanted to be a daughter of Eve.

Now, I understand. Lewis was warning us. We are all daughters of Eve (or sons of Adam) whether we want to be or not. We have all inherited their tendency to be led astray. And there is still a snake in the grass.

How much sweeter our lives would be, the Enemy croons, if we would follow him instead of the One whom he attempts to paint as a cruel and hard taskmaster. When Satan and Eve had their exchange in the garden, they stopped calling God "Lord God" (*Yahweh Elohim*), which He is called sixteen times in Genesis 2 and 3, and call Him simply "God" (*Elohim*, meaning Creator). In the *Word Biblical Commentary*, Gordon Wenham explains that Satan, and then Eve, dropped *Yahweh*, the Jewish national name for God, because that term expresses the goodness of God and the fact that He is our loving covenant partner. "The god they are describing," Wenham says, "is malevolent, secretive, and concerned to restrict man."[2]

Satan wants us to *forget* the goodness of God. He lies, "If you obey God, you will be **miserable**." Then, when he has our attention, he beckons, cooing: "Come, **I** can give you Turkish Delight. Try a bite." As the first morsel is melting in our mouths, he beguiles: "I have plenty more. If you will just sell out your family and friends, I will give you more!"

Beth Moore, in *A Woman's Heart: God's Dwelling Place*, believes Satan targeted Eve because he knew how influential she could be as a woman. Beth believes that God has created women with a unique power of influence, and it is a gift. We know how to please, to coax, and to sway those close to us. "We can use our gift of influence outside of the Spirit and be dangerous," Beth cautions. "Guard your gift."[3]

There are intriguing parallels in the story of Eve and the story of Sarah. What got them both into trouble? *They forgot the goodness of God.* Then they both led their husbands astray. They both tried to pass the blame, and both husbands were rebuked for obeying their wives without checking with God. We have enormous influence, as women, for good or for evil, and so it makes sense that Satan would target us. He knows if he can deceive us, we will often spread the lie to our husbands and friends. He hopes we will take our children by the hand and lead them down the path toward destruction. It makes sense to slither toward the *relational sex*. Why aim for just one when you can have a whole family?

The Becklers' story parallels the story of Adam and Eve and Abraham and Sarah in an uncanny way. With all three couples, God came to them and told them His good plan. Next, the Enemy appeared and slithered toward the woman. Rolling his eyes, he whispered, "Did God really say?"

Did God really say, Eve, that you must not eat from any tree in the garden? Surely, you won't die!

Did God really say, Sarah, that you would give birth to a son? Surely, you are too old!

After God came to Lori and Bob and interrupted them, impressing on their hearts to do a women's conference, they had a period of excited expectancy about what God was going to do. Perhaps Satan was waiting to see if they were truly serious before he chose to attack.

STEPS OF FAITH: DECEMBER 27, 1995

When God begins to lead, there is a sense of expectancy in the air. When the phone rings, when you look at your e-mail, when you cross paths with someone, you wonder, *Lord, are you giving me another piece of the puzzle?* Often women are the first to believe: our gift of women's intuition equips us to spot God on the move. That happened with Bob and Lori a few days after Christmas.

On December 27, Bob and Lori were in the midst of talking about plans for the women's conference when the phone rang. Bob explained: "It was the secretary for the senior pastor of a huge church in town: Central Community. She asked me if I could schedule an appointment with Senior Pastor John Henry that next week. My first reaction was, *Oh great—this is probably about some problem with the school,* because Trinity Academy (where I was administrator and coach) was renting space from them. But when I got off the phone and told Lori who it was, she said:

I bet he wants to talk to you about a job.

"Then there was a moment of silence and I looked at her, amazed, and said, **What?**

"She shrugged: *Bob—I don't know where that came from.*"

The seed, however, was planted in Bob's mind. By the time he walked through Central Community's foyer on January 2, it was with a spirit of anticipation. Before Bob opened the door to Pastor John Henry's office, he breathed this prayer: *Lord, I just want to be open to hear what You want me to do.*

Pastor John Henry said, "Bob, what do you see yourself doing in the next three, four, five years?"

Bob took a deep breath, amazed at his wife's intuition, and said, "John, you're going to talk to me about coming here to work at the church, aren't you?"

John nodded and said, "Yes."

Reflectively, Bob told me: "That was a confirmation to me that Lori and I were each being called, that we were together in this, and that somehow, Central Community was another piece in the puzzle. At that point, I said in my own heart: *Lord, I don't know what You are going to do, but I will follow You every step of the way.*"

Bob left his position at Trinity Academy and took a ministry position at Central Community, in obedient faith. Central Community Church *was* a key part of God's plan. It hosted the first Heritage Keepers conference, was an invaluable resource for speakers, and equipped Bob, as he engineered follow-up for the Franklin Graham Crusade, to engineer follow-up for future Heritage Keepers conferences. Bob was moving up the mountain step-by-step on faith.

When God is leading, and His children are following, usually an enemy lurks in the shadows. I like the way the authors of *The Sacred Romance* phrase this: "Something wonderful woos us, but something fearful stalks us."[4]

Bob and Lori had shown themselves to be serious about following God's plan. It was time for Satan to make his move.

TURKISH DELIGHT OFFERED: JANUARY 19, 1996

After the holidays, Lori went back to work at the travel and convention office to find her desk piled high and the phone ringing off the hook. Bob speaks glowingly of his wife, explaining why so many people wanted her to make their travel plans or to book their conventions:

> *Like her dad, Lori is such a hard worker, gives so much attention to detail, and genuinely cares for her customers. No one could match her. I'm not surprised that more and more opportunities were coming her way.*

I have heard it said that if Satan can't make us bad, he'll make us busy. (How often do we neglect the Word of God or ignore God's still small voice because of the tyranny of the urgent? There is a reason God admonishes us to live quiet lives.) Certainly Lori was busy. She said: "I pushed the women's conference over to one side because the demands of the world were taking over. I wasn't seeking more conventions to book, they were coming to me. One particularly hectic Friday I had a morning, a lunch, and an afternoon meeting with a group of powerful men who wanted me to book five large conventions for them. Everything was moving so smoothly, and it was clear the financial rewards were going to be huge. The heady feeling of power was alluring. I came out of the lunch meeting on such a high—but it wasn't a God high, it was a Lori high. I was thinking: *Look how successful I am, look how much confidence these powerful businessmen have in me, look at how much money I am going to make.*" Visions of Turkish Delight.

Satan doesn't have a lot of tricks, but the three he has have worked so well through the ages, he just keeps pulling the same old Turkish Delight out of his bag. He beckons with:

> *The lust of the flesh (the desire for food, sex, etc.).*
>
> *The lust of the eyes (the desire for houses, cars, clothes, etc.).*

The pride of life (prestige positions for self, spouse, children; popularity, the general desire to be important, beautiful, etc.).

He tempted Eve with all three (see Genesis 3:6). With Lori he tried the last two, to lure her off the path. "That afternoon," Lori told me, shaking her head, "God gave me such a warning sign—but I didn't heed it."

"What was it?" I asked.

Lori clasped her arms around her knees and put her head down, remembering that afternoon meeting. Looking up, she said, "Two of the men got into a power struggle. Though this was a meeting that called for some class, they began to use foul language, swear words, escalating their profanity like punches in a boxing match, trying to be the one in control. Though they knew I was a Christian, and a woman, they showed no respect for my presence. I felt degraded."

Jesus said that out of the overflow of the heart the mouth speaks, and bile was flowing on that January afternoon. God gave Lori a second warning sign after work, for when she relayed this scene to Bob, he was shocked. Lori said, "I'll never forget the way he looked at me when he said, 'Lori—why did you let them talk to you like that?'"

Bob said, "To me, it was a huge red flag. I was so offended. I wanted to call those guys and say, 'How dare you use that kind of language in front of my wife!' But Lori kept saying, 'Don't worry about it—don't worry about it—I can handle them.' Even the way she said that was another red flag to me. I thought, *Why is this account so important?* Lori had always said to me, 'Bob, when we make decisions, we don't ever have to take money into account—because God will take care of us.' So why, now, though the money was good, was she not simply shutting the door on these guys?"

Brushing Bob's concerns aside, Lori began to fix supper. Still excited about the enormous opportunity being offered to her, she called her mother, Betty, and told her about "the exciting events of the day." Lori also mentioned to her mom how the men had talked in front of her, and Betty had the same shocked reaction as Bob. "Lori—why did you let them talk like that in front of you? Why didn't you take a stand?"

Despite the fact that God confirmed His warning through Lori's husband and mother, Lori wasn't ready to plug her ears to Satan. She wanted to keep her hands on the Turkish Delight. As often happens when we are tempted by the Enemy, we rationalize, hoping to justify our position and thereby avoid the cost of following Christ. Lori ignored each blinking warning sign and kept walking down the path toward the Turkish Delight, rationalizing: *Pretty soon these guys will be out of my life. After I land the account, I will ask to work with a man in this firm whom I know to be a Christian, and I won't have to put up with these guys anymore.*

DON'T GIVE SATAN A FOOTHOLD

All Satan wants is a foot in the door. The Turkish Delight is meant to entice us to open the door a crack. If we don't heed God's still small voice and shut the door, but just take a peek, the White Witch sticks a bony foot in, crashes through, and fills the room with her evil presence. She is in charge! As Lewis so picturesquely portrays, she slips her harness over our surprised shoulders and cracks her whip on our tender back. We soon discover we have been deceived, for it is really she, not Jesus, who is the cruel and hard taskmaster.

I am convinced that God is entreating us, as His daughters, to listen to Him, to remember that He is good, not evil, and to teach our children about His praiseworthy deeds, so that they will understand that God is good, and not evil, and will trust Him:

O my people, hear my teaching;
listen to the words of my mouth.
I will open my mouth in parables,
I will utter hidden things, things from of old—
what we have heard and known,
what our fathers have told us.
We will not hide them from their children;
we will tell the next generation

the praiseworthy deeds of the Lord,
his power, and the wonders he has done. (Psalm 78:1-4)

As mothers, our power of influence is immense. When Eve failed to remember that God was good, she not only brought incredible pain to herself and to her husband, but to her children, for the sins of the parents are passed down to the next generation. We tend to follow in the footsteps of our parents. Just as Satan beguiled Eve, he beguiled her son, Cain.

Cain was jealous of his brother, Abel, for Abel had pleased God and Cain had not. Read carefully God's loving warning to Cain:

Then the Lord said to Cain, "Why are you angry? Why is your face downcast? If you do what is right, will you not be accepted? But if you do not do what is right, sin is crouching at your door; it desires to have you, but you must master it." (Genesis 4:6-7)

Satan tells us we will be unhappy if we obey God. What a deception! Though it is true that there may be some initial pain in obeying God, it will actually lead to joy and peace—not unhappiness. God *will* lift us up. He would have done that for Cain had Cain heeded His warning. Instead, Cain didn't listen, Satan got a foothold, and Cain went out and murdered his brother.

It has been helpful to me, every day, when I am tempted, to realize my choices. Think about this today when you are tempted. You can either:

Endure the initial pain of saying no to sin and be lifted up
or
Flirt with sin, give Satan a foothold, and be overpowered.

God's warning to Cain contains a word picture. In the *Word Biblical Commentary*, Gordon Wenham explains: "sin is personified as a demon crouching like a wild beast on Cain's doorstep."[5] Imagine that beast snarling the next time you are tempted to ignore the soft prompting of the Spirit! Sin is no friend. Obeying the pull of sin gives initial gratification, but it will actually lead to feeling angry and downcast. The Turkish Delight turns rancid. When should we refuse Satan? The *moment* we recognize him, for he is crouching at the door, seizing any lapse as an opportunity to get a foothold. The desire of sin and of Satan is to "have you," that is, literally in the Hebrew, "to stretch over or to dominate you." (This is the Hebrew word *shuquah*. You will see it again soon in a vital passage for husbands and wives.)

When should Lori have shut the door? The moment she recognized the Enemy. She opened the door a crack at the sight of the Turkish Delight and then hesitated. Even when God warned her through her husband and mother, she procrastinated letting go of the Turkish Delight. Satan was firmly in. Now it was going to take a battle, and some help from her loved ones, to get him out.

THE SPIRITUAL BATTLE: JANUARY 19, 1996

After supper, Lori drove her children and their friends to another basketball game. "It was an away game," Lori remembered, "and my mind was cranking all the way to the game, blocking out the chatter in a car full of middle schoolers. I was thinking, *Wow, this is going to be great. The money is going to be unbelievable.* The Holy Spirit was whispering, but I was shouting Him down."

> *Lori, how are you going to handle five conventions and still work part time—still be there for your husband and kids?*
>
> **I can do it. One of the conventions is in Orlando—Bob and Nicole and Daniel can come with me. It will be a family vacation on the side. Lord, You know I value my family. I'm not going to hurt my family. I still want to work part time. I think I can get it all done and still work part time. And wow, it will be great.**
>
> *Lori, what about the women's conference? Were you serious about that?*
>
> **There's no money in that, just a whole lot of risk.**
>
> *Lori, where is your focus?*

I don't want to think about that right now.

Before you judge Lori, I want you to appreciate that stepping out on faith and doing the women's conference was a *huge* challenge, and we should not minimize the stretch. When Lori was working for the convention business, they provided the funds and told her what to do, whereas doing a Christian conference meant that Lori and Bob would have to trust God for the enormous financial outlay as well as the assignments. Walking by faith feels much riskier than walking by sight. When doubts and fears begin to plague you, the most natural response in the world is to retreat.

In John Bunyan's *Pilgrim's Progress*, Christian sets out in his journey toward the Celestial City. One of his first experiences is to fall into the "slough of despond," that miry place early in a journey where doubts and fears settle! Christian's companion, Pliable, falls into the slough as well, is offended, and retreats. But Christian, despite the discouraging beginning, persists. Soon God lifts him up and gives him joy in the journey.

After God confirmed His leading to Bob and Lori, they fell into the "slough of despond." When they began to call various sources looking for help, people seemed unable to give them support. They felt stuck, unable to proceed. It is often at *this* crucial point that Satan comes sliding in, hissing through his forked tongue: Did God really say? The doubts begin to pile up. *Perhaps we imagined His leading. Why is this journey getting so difficult?* Many, like Pliable, will retreat at this point.

Something wonderful woos us, but something fearful stalks us. By the time Lori and her children got to the game that night, she was in a daze. "We were seated on the bleachers," Lori remembered, "Nicole on one side, Daniel on the other—and I didn't feel quite right. Light headed—in a fog. I thought, *Maybe I didn't eat enough for supper.* I asked Nicole to go to the concession stand with me. I nibbled on some popcorn, but I couldn't push the fog away. I saw our friends Suzi and Randy Storms and asked them if I could sit with them. I told them I didn't feel quite right. I'm not sick, but I feel like I'm in a dream.'"

Concerned, Suzi asked: "Are you having a panic attack?"

Lori headed for the restroom. Leaning on the sink, her head down, she prayed. "Lord, what is going on? What is the matter with me?" The moment Lori prayed, God spoke to her—in that still small voice, through her thoughts:

> *Lori, you are just feeling so good about yourself. You think you can do this and you can do that and work your family around it. In the snap of My fingers I can take it all away. You think you are in control of your life, but you are not at all. You are on a Lori high. What about the women's conference? Where is your focus going to be? Are you going to love the world or are you going to love Me?*

Lori walked back into the gym. "During the rest of the game I kept trying to shake myself from the fog, but I couldn't. I went to Bob after the game and told him I didn't trust myself to drive the kids home. Though I knew he was responsible for driving the van and getting all these basketball players home, I needed him."

Bob said, "There was a time when that request, considering my responsibility, would have irritated me, but I knew something was going on, something bigger than Lori and me, and I needed to be there for her. All the way home Lori kept saying, 'I'm sorry, I'm sorry,' but I really wasn't upset because I could see that God was doing something and that she was going through some real spiritual turmoil."

I can't be sure what was happening with Lori, but I sense it was a genuine spiritual battle. When Jacob wrestled with the angel it was a spiritual battle: who was going to be in control? Jacob or God? Jacob had gone the way of the world his whole life, but God wanted to wrest him from the Enemy because Jacob was *His heritage*. That battle left Jacob with the physical scar of a limp. Spiritual battles can lead to physical symptoms. Jacob, unlike Cain, listened to God in the midst of his pain. Jacob, unlike Cain, held onto God until he received a blessing.

Jacob, unlike Cain, humbled himself before his brother. God blessed Jacob mightily, reconciling him with his brother, among other things. What a contrast to Cain, who murdered his brother and became a fugitive on earth. Charles Spurgeon says that when we sense we are in a spiritual battle we must ask: "Lord, why are you contending with me?"

God got Lori's attention that night. When she and Bob and the children got home, they all put on their pajamas and Lori made some popcorn. God, in His mercy, was opening Lori's eyes to the deceit of the Turkish Delight. Lori said, "I was in tears as the four of us cozied together in front of TV with a bowl of popcorn. I told the Lord silently, *Lord, this is all I want. I don't need all those worldly things. I don't care about those things. I just want to be where You want me to be. I want You to be in control.*

Lori then went to bed and slept peacefully.

MY DAUGHTER, MY DAUGHTER, INCLINE YOUR EAR

God entreats us, as women, to listen to Him. He longs for us to look back to our holy heritage and to understand the hidden pictures He has painted for us in the Old Testament. The Old Testament is like a golden storybook of illustrations, and the New Testament often provides the captions.

In the letters of John, the Apostle John provides the captions for the Old Testament story of Cain.

> *This is the message you heard from the beginning: We should love one another. Do not be like Cain, who belonged to the evil one and murdered his brother. And why did he murder him? Because his own actions were evil and his brother's were righteous....*
>
> *Dear children, let us not love with words or tongue but with actions and in truth. This then is how we know that we belong to the truth, and how we set our hearts at rest in his presence.* (1 John 3:11-12, 18-19)

The key test to know if we are in the light is to look at our relationship with others. Is there harmony and real love in your home? Is your relationship with your friends or coworkers peaceful and encouraging? If not, it is likely your relationship with God is in need of repair.

THE LIGHT SHINES IN THE SHOWER: JANUARY 20, 1996

It makes me laugh to realize how often God speaks to us in the shower. Maybe it is because, if we are mothers, it is one of the few places where we can really be alone! Maybe it is because the cares of the world are so much with us that we need that steady stream of hot water to wash them away, to relax our tense muscles, and to help us reflect, in that silent, secluded chamber, on what really matters in life.

When my sister Sally was teaching Spanish at Iowa State, a freshman girl asked her, "Mrs. Frahm, is there any reason you couldn't give your life to Jesus Christ?" It was in the shower that that question came back to haunt Sally.

I often have moments of illumination for my writing in the shower. A year ago I pled with God, in the shower at our cabin, to show me the backbone for this book. After months of running down a labyrinth of paths that led to frustrating dead ends, He showed me, as I was rinsing shampoo from my hair, how simple it could be. *Sarah.* She and Abraham were the beginning of our holy heritage. From them tumbled generation after generation of believers. Pictures began to come to my head of holy women of old: Sarah, Rebekah, Jochebed....I began to sway in the shower, lifting my arms, one at a time, to that catchy chorus that has preschoolers turning round and round without comprehension of the great truth they are singing:

Father Abraham had many sons
Many sons had Father Abraham
I am one of them, and so are you
So let's just praise the Lord.

Having just completed the manuscript *A Woman's Journey Through 1 Peter,* I also thought about Peter's promise that we can become Sarah's daughters if we do what is right and don't give way to hysterical fears.

(1 Peter 3:6 J.B. PHILLIPS) The puzzle was coming together. *This, Dee,* I sensed the Spirit saying, *is your holy heritage. Show these hidden pictures to My daughters.*

When Lori awoke on that Saturday morning and stepped into the shower, she had an experience that helped her to usher the Enemy out and to return to the path to which God had called her. I'll tell you this wonderful story in the next chapter—but first, be sure to do the Bible study so that you know how to shut the door on the Enemy. He is lurking in the shadows, but you must master him.

Panning for Heritage Gold

☼ Icebreaker: Give an example of Turkish Delight that beckons to you and one which has no allure. (I have to resist the desire to be popular, but a lottery ticket leaves me cold.)

Meditate: We are less tempted in those areas in which we are less deceived.

1. What stood out to you from the text and Scriptures in the third chapter? Why?

Read 1 John 2:15-17.

2. What strong statement does John make in verse 15?

How was this exemplified in Lori's battle between doing the secular conferences and the women's conference?

3. Note that when John specifies the categories of temptations he calls them cravings or lusts. What is the difference between thankfully receiving a good thing God gives you and lusting after it?

Give an example of how lust can turn a good thing into sin.

4. What are the three categories of temptation? Give an example of each.

Find each category in Satan's temptation of Eve in Genesis 3:6.

5. What evidence can you find for Eve forgetting God's goodness?

Find each category in Satan's temptation of Jesus in Matthew 4:1-11.

What did Jesus do to resist Satan?

6. List a common temptation for you. Prepare a Scripture to use as a sword, in your defense, when Satan beckons. (A few possibilities are: Genesis 4:7; 2 Samuel 22:26; Matthew 4:10; 1 Peter 2:9-11. Or, ask God to show you one.) Memorize it so your sword is ready to strike!

7. Why, according to 1 John 2:17, should we always choose the path of loving God instead of loving the world?

☀ Read Genesis 2:15-25.

I find it interesting that after each of these covenants the Enemy stalked the woman, and she persuaded her husband to do wrong.

Read Genesis 3:1-17.

8. Whom did Adam blame for his sin? (v. 12) Whom did Eve blame? (v. 13)

9. What does God tell the woman? (v. 16) (We'll study this phrase more carefully in Chapter 4.)

10. If you are married, do you habitually try to manipulate or dominate your husband to get your way? Why is this displeasing to God?

11. What did Adam do that was displeasing to God? (Genesis 3:17)

In the *Word Biblical Commentary*, Gordon Wenham shows, in the Hebrew, that the phrase "listened to the voice" is repeated only in Genesis 16:2, where Abraham listened to the voice of Sarah.[6] The warning is not that husbands shouldn't listen to their wives, for later God tells Abraham *to listen to Sarah*, but that they should check with God for confirmation.

12. As a woman, you have a gift of influence. Be still before God and ask Him to show you areas in which you are using your gift wisely and areas in which you are dangerous. List them.

☼ Read Genesis 4:1-7.

13. Describe the two choices God gave Cain.

What would be the consequences of each? Have you experienced this? Explain.

What word picture does God give of sin or of Satan?

14. Giving into any kind of temptation gives Satan a foothold. A few common ways that Satan gets a foothold are described in the following passages. What are they? What do they mean?

    A. 1 Corinthians 7:1-5

    B. Ephesians 4:26-27

    C. Hebrews 12:15

Satan tells us God is a cruel taskmaster, that He only wants to limit us. Remember, God is good and He loves you. It is Satan who is the cruel taskmaster.

15. God wants us to be "against forgetting." What gold have you discovered that has given you fresh understanding? (When we understand, it is less likely we will forget.) How will you apply it to your life?

PRAYER TIME:

Lift up your answer to question 14 or another need in your life in prayer and allow a few sisters to support you with a sentence prayer. Then another woman should do the same.

Four

When there is a problem in your horizontal relationship, it is almost always because there is a problem in your vertical relationship with God. Sort that out, and your marriage will again become the harmonious oneness that God intended.

PASTOR PAUL KUPFERSCHMID AT THE WEDDING OF JEREMIE SOLAK AND SALLY BRESTIN IN EPHRAIM, WISCONSIN ON JULY 26, 1997

A Heritage of Harmony

When Lori stepped into the shower that Saturday morning, warm water and childhood memories washed over her, causing her to weep. "Clips of me as a child flooded my mind. When I was just a little girl I would pull my mom's black half-slip over my neck and pretend I was a preacher. Standing on a box in front of the mirror, I'd tell the imaginary crowd all about Jesus. All I wanted to do when I grew up was to let people know about how wonderful He is. Then I pictured myself playing the guitar as a teenager at church, singing my heart out for the Lord. I remembered the feeling of excitement, of what was most important in life. All I wanted to do when I grew up was to share who God was with people. I wept to realize how I had lost that first love. I sensed that God was saying to me: *Lori, why don't you just step out on faith for this conference? If only a couple hundred women come, if only one woman's life is changed between hell and heaven, wouldn't that be worth it? Won't you just trust Me? I'll provide everything you need.* Lori turned off the shower, reached for a towel, and stepped out of the tub. Overwhelmed by the Spirit of God, she sank to her knees, sobbing.

Bob said, "I woke up, and the bathroom door was closed, and I heard Lori crying. And she wasn't just crying, she was *weeping*. I opened the door to find her curled up in a fetal position next to the tub, mascara running down her cheeks."

Instantly he crouched his large frame next to her small one, pulling her to himself, cradling her, rocking her: "Lori, Lori—are you okay? Talk to me. What's going on?"

After a few moments, between sobs, Lori whispered, "I'm not sure what God is doing, but I know that I want to be used by Him. Whatever He wants."

"Yes, yes, Lori." Bob bundled Lori more tightly in his arms, trying to still her trembling.

After a few moments Lori calmed. Taking a deep breath, she felt a new determination. "God wants us to do this conference. I've pushed it aside, I've gotten off the path, but . . . no more. I need to call those men who want me to do all those secular conventions and say no."

Together, in the bathroom, they knelt and surrendered everything again to God: their lives, their ministry—everything. Together they submitted themselves to the will of God, enjoying the wonderful oneness that brings. They would step out on faith, one step at a time, trusting that God would provide. Bob said, "God broke my wife, right before my eyes. When we knelt together, surrendering anew to Him, I felt a tenderness—as though Someone had His arms around us."

The picture of Bob and Lori kneeling together, being enfolded in the arms of God is a beautiful portrait of the oneness God intended for marriage. The only way we can have that sweet harmonious oneness is to examine our individual relationships with God.

If you are single please stay with us, because this chapter is going to be relevant for you. Denise, of Point of Grace, shared with the Heritage Keepers audience in Wichita that God had prepared her for marriage through the ups and downs of her friendship with Heather,

Terry, and Shelley. She tickled me when she said, "I knew I was ready to be married, because I'd already been married." I knew exactly what she meant. I remember telling our daughter Sally that if she couldn't get along with her freshman roommate in college, she would have trouble getting along with her future husband. Learning to get along with other people, whether they are your girlfriends, your mother, or your husband—is something that occurs because of spiritual growth.

The desire to dominate in order to get our own way isn't just confined to marriage: that sad effect of the Fall is the primary cause of strife in all human relationships. It is a warning that we have left the path of God and are following our own way. We have stopped listening. We are beginning to wander in the wilderness—and squabbling all the way. But our heritage, if we go back to the garden before the Fall, was sweet fellowship: with God, and with one another, whether it is our marriage partner or a sister in Christ.

There is a secret to recovering that heritage of harmony, but you need to look below the surface in the scriptural text.

THE DESIRE TO DOMINATE

Do you remember how God warned Cain that "sin was crouching at the door, and *desired* to have him?" This "desire to stretch over or to dominate" is the Hebrew word *shuquah*. This "desire to dominate" is one of the sad effects of the fall, marring God's original plan for oneness in marriage. Instead of a couple submitting to God and walking in harmony, now they each would desire their own selfish way. Each would "desire to dominate" (*shuquah*) the other to get his or her own way. God explained this when He came to Adam and Eve after they had sinned and listed the consequences, the effects of the Fall. Among those, He explained to Eve, was:

> *Your desire will be for your husband, and he will rule over you.* (Genesis 3:16b)

Some have considered that the "desire" in Genesis 3:16b might mean "sexual desire," pointing out that in the Song of Solomon 7:10, the desire, or the stretching out, is for physical intimacy:

I belong to my lover,
and his desire is for me.

However, if that was the intended interpretation, we would have to conclude that sexual desire was a negative effect of the Fall, and that certainly does not agree with the rest of Scripture. Consider, for example, Proverbs 5:18-19:

May you rejoice in the wife of your youth.
A loving doe, a graceful deer—
may her breasts satisfy you always,
may you ever be captivated by her love.

Or consider the refrains describing the ecstasy of married lovemaking in the Song of Solomon, or the clear word of the Lord in Hebrews 13:4:

Marriage is honourable in all, and the bed undefiled. (KJV)

The sexual relationship in marriage is a blessed gift from God, and it was present before the Fall. (Consider Adam's ecstatic reaction when he met Eve!)

Therefore, I am convinced the "desire" in Genesis 3:16 is not sexual desire, but the "desire to dominate" as it is used concerning sin's "desire to dominate" Cain in Genesis 4:7. Henceforth women would desire to dominate their husbands, and husbands, in return, would harshly rule over their wives. Instead of loving harmony, there would be manipulation on the part of the wife and a reaction of insensitive domination on the part of the husband. This strife was not God's plan. His plan was that "the two would be one." The effects of the Fall can only be reversed as we submit to Christ.

GOD'S BLUEPRINT FOR MARRIAGE: THE TWO SHALL BE ONE

I am amazed at the wonderful creativity of our God, to make the sexual relationship such a beautiful picture of what He intended marriage to be in every sense: not only physically, but emotionally and spiritually. Certainly the world has missed this picture as it has abused and distorted the gift of sex. Even we, though we are believers, still see as through a glass darkly, glimpsing only part of God's glorious picture of marriage. As many times as I have read and meditated on the poetry of Genesis 2:22-24, I know I only understand in part:

> *Then the Lord God made a woman from the rib he had taken out of the man, and he brought her to the man.*
> *The man said,*
> *"This is now bone of my bones*
> *and flesh of my flesh;*
> *she shall be called 'woman,'*
> *for she was taken out of man."*
> *For this reason a man will leave his father and mother and be united to his wife, and they will become one flesh.*

One of the ways to discover God's hidden truths is to look for patterns in Scriptures, and certainly the overwhelming pattern for marriage is not, "Who's in charge here?" but "The two shall become one."

When the Pharisees came to Jesus asking Him if divorce was lawful, Jesus was grieved, saying that was never God's original plan, but that Moses permitted it because of "the hardness of men's hearts." Notice how Jesus refers to God's plan for marriage before the Fall.

> *"It was because your hearts were hard that Moses wrote you this law,"* *Jesus replied. "But at the beginning of creation God 'made them male and female.' 'For this reason a man will leave his father and mother and be united to his wife, and the two will become one flesh.' So they are no longer two, but one. Therefore what God has joined together, let man not separate." (Mark 10:5-9)*

The prophet Malachi thunders against God's people, because they have forgotten the importance of oneness in marriage. They can't understand why God is not answering their prayers. Malachi explains they have forgotten something that is so precious to God:

You flood the Lord's altar with tears. You weep and wail because he no longer pays attention to your offerings or accepts them with pleasure from your hands. You ask, "Why?" It is because the Lord is acting as the witness between you and the wife of your youth, because you have broken faith with her, though she is your partner, the wife of your marriage covenant. Has not the Lord made them one? In flesh and spirit they are his. And why one? Because he was seeking godly offspring. So guard yourself in your spirit, and do not break faith with the wife of your youth. (Malachi 2:13-15)

Did you see, in the above, one of the reasons God has made a man and wife one? *Because he was seeking godly offspring.* Part of passing on a godly heritage to the next generation demands that we preserve this harmony. Not only do we refrain from divorce, but we seek to be physically, spiritually, and emotionally one.

Likewise, one of the reasons infidelity is such an abomination to God is that it violates the oneness of marriage. This is why Paul says, in 1 Corinthians 6:16:

Do you not know that he who unites himself with a prostitute is one with her in body? For it is said, "The two will become one flesh."

And later, Ephesians 5:21-31 is a key passage showing all believers how to reverse selfishness and to live, not divided, but harmoniously. First, Paul opens, in verse 21, with a summary command to all believers:

Submit to one another out of reverence for Christ.

Then he goes on to specifically address the marriage relationship. He urges wives to submit to their husbands (rather than to desire to dominate them) and urges husbands to gently, and in a spirit of servanthood, lead their wives (rather than to harshly rule them).

Wives, submit to your husbands as to the Lord....
Husbands, love your wives, just as Christ loved the church and gave himself up for her....

The only way we can return to God's original blueprint of oneness is to overcome *shuquah*, that selfish desire to get our own way, and submit to one another out of reverence for Christ.

HARMONY IN MARRIAGE

Instead of a wife manipulating and coaxing her husband in order to get her own way, she should put her trust in God, and ask God to put His desire in her husband's heart. Usually a believing couple can become like-minded in Christ. But if they cannot, then she should submit to her husband (unless he is asking her to sin), trusting that God is at work. You may ask, how can I possibly do that? You can do that by remembering how God bent down and blessed His children as they obeyed Him in the past, and believe He will do that for you still today.

The husband, instead of responding to a wife's manipulation with an iron hand, should lead gently, as Christ did, should think of her needs, as Christ did, and should serve her, as Christ did. A husband may ask, how can I possibly do that? Won't she take advantage of me? A husband can do that by remembering how God bent down and blessed His children as they obeyed Him in the past, and believe He will do that still today.

Marriage is one of the ways God is molding us, conforming us to the image of Christ. In a mysterious way, marriage is a reflection of a bigger picture, that of Christ and the church. As we learn to become one in marriage, we are also being prepared to be the bride of Christ. For Paul continues in Ephesians 5:32:

> This is a profound mystery—but I am talking about Christ and the church.

It's an amazing hidden picture.

Becoming one is a process, and some fight it all the way, like the pot that wants to jump off the potter's wheel. Being molded can be painful, but how I long to tell younger women that it will be worth it. When I contrast the early years of our marriage to where Steve and I are today, it's like the difference between sleeping on a gunny sack and 370-count fine Egyptian cotton. Marriage is such a welcome haven. It is exciting, yet at the same time smooth and soothing. I cannot wait until he comes home. My heart leaps when I run into him. The last true argument I remember was fifteen years ago. I thank God, over and over and over again, for the great joy in our marriage. We pray, we laugh, we love. We are spiritually, emotionally, and physically one. What a contrast to the early years!

SLEEPING ON A SCRATCHY GUNNYSACK

As a newlywed I was petulant and selfish, desiring my own way, and desiring to manipulate and dominate my husband into giving it to me. How I remember our first Christmas, a time when God refined us both, smoothing away the jagged edges that were keeping us from becoming one.

All I wanted to do was to go home, and for me, home was still Mom and Dad. There I would be pampered again, as I had always been. There we would have a white Wisconsin Christmas. There, and only there, I was convinced, could we truly have Christmas. How could we have Christmas in Indiana, where it was raining?

All Steve wanted to do was to stay in Indiana and study. He was in medical school and was behind. He hadn't been feeling well and was overwhelmed with work. He had agreed to go to Wisconsin for a little while, but wanted to hurry back to study. A clash of two wills: neither of us wanted to submit to the other, and if someone had told us we needed to submit our wills to God it would have been like Swahili to us. My plan was to get us to Wisconsin and then manipulate my husband into staying longer than originally planned.

Then God allowed us to go through a crisis. Though this will astonish those who know Steve now, in his pre-Christ days he smoked two-and-a-half packs of Camels a day. (Later, the power of Christ strengthened Steve to give up smoking completely overnight.) Smoking, which certainly isn't what those lying advertisements of healthy outdoorsmen or classy women make it out to be, was killing my twenty-year-old husband. The cigarettes, coupled with the stress of medical school, had made him much sicker than either of us realized. We thought he was coming down with the flu. (I was angry—how dare he be so careless as to get the flu just before Christmas? Was he really sick—or was he trying to get his own way and keep us from going to Wisconsin?) As the day progressed, he doubled up in pain and turned gray. I called an ambulance and sat waiting for news in the hospital waiting room. Still, uppermost in my mind was not my husband's health, but the fear that we would not be going home for Christmas. An older doctor brought me to my senses when he came out and told me that Steve had severe pericarditis (an infection of the lining of the heart with complications) and might not live. Suddenly, what was important in life became quite clear. We would not be going to Wisconsin, and that was okay. I just wanted my husband to live.

Meanwhile, God was working on Steve. As he struggled for breath in that large intensive care ward, two other patients were struggling as well. One, right next to him, went frightened and yelling through the icy river of death. Steve was sobered, and his mind began to ponder eternity. The young man on the other side of Steve, though he had a congenital heart problem and was facing a surgery with a 50 percent fatality rate, was calm and peaceful. When Steve asked him how he could be so calm, the man said: "It is because I have put my trust in Christ, and I know He is waiting to meet me at the other side." That was the first glimpse Steve had of genuine Christianity.

That following fall Steve and I put our trust in Christ and began to grow in Him. As the years passed and we learned, more and more, what it meant to die to self and to live to Christ, God changed the discordant sounds of our marriage into a harmonious symphony. Christ has reversed the effects of the Fall in our marriage—we are truly one. When we disagreed, our approach to conflict became entirely different.

SLEEPING ON FINE EGYPTIAN COTTON

Before her husband Harold's death, Luci Shaw told me: "Harold is the head of our home, and I submit to him. But in thirty years of marriage, it has only come up twice."

I must admit that I have had to submit more than twice, but it has been relatively rare. Steve has often submitted to my desires, and sometimes I was right (as in desiring a third child) and sometimes I was wrong (as in desiring a playhouse for our daughters, which they completely avoided because of the bugs). Most frequently when we disagree, we seek God's face, and He gives us a like-mindedness. We are often amazed, for example, how we will pray about something, such as a sum to give a missionary, and will come together to discover we have the exact same idea. How exciting to have the God who made the universe bend down and whisper the same thing to each of us. This harmony is like sleeping on fine Egyptian cotton.

Yet, there have been times when, after prayer, we have not agreed. Steve has not felt led to submit to me, so I must submit to him. Most frequently, that has had to do with moving. I am impressed that Sarah sojourned as sweetly as she did, for it is difficult to leave your friends, family, church, and home. (We'll look at Sarah more carefully later, but suffice it to say now that we are told that the secret of Sarah's submission and her lack of fear had to do with her faith in God. She had seen God bless obedience, and she did not forget what He could do.)

One of the most difficult moves for me occurred when Steve, after being in a medical practice for four years, wanted to uproot and "go back to school" by taking a year of unrequired internal medicine training. ("You're already the best," I argued. "How many surgeons take extra training in internal medicine?") It meant leaving Seattle, most glorious of cities, for Fargo, North Dakota, most inglorious (or so I unfairly thought) of cities. It meant uprooting our children, two of whom were in their teens, for one year, and then uprooting them again. I wanted to wrap my arms around the furniture and say, "No! Never!" But it became clear to me that we were not going to be like-minded, and this was going to be a case in which I would need to submit. Why? So that our marriage would be a "Christian unity." (Colossians 3:18b J.B. PHILLIPS)

One of the greatest blessings we can give our children is that of a harmony between their mother and father. Will your husband always be right? No, but God will bless you for trusting Him enough to submit to your husband. (Our move to Fargo, though not without pain for us or our children, yielded many wonderful blessings, including one of the best churches we've ever known, wonderful friends, training for Steve which has equipped him to spot heart disease and cancer in some of his orthopedic patients, and, most importantly, a marriage that is a Christian unity.)

Sometimes a young woman will ask me, "What if you have sought God's face and your husband has not? Do you still have to submit to him?" Recently, at a women's conference a young woman said: "My husband wants to buy a Mercedes, and I feel that would be neither good stewardship nor a good witness. He hasn't really sought God's face. He's just doing what he wants to do. Do I have to submit to this?" I told her that I thought she had a responsibility to gently and clearly submit any Scriptures or leadings she had to her husband, for that is our role as a coheir. (Many Christian wives just bail out, leaving their husbands to make the whole decision, and then blame them for poor results.) However, after she had submitted her thoughts, if they were still at loggerheads, then she needed to submit. And not only did she need to submit, she needed to do it without bitterness. Why? So that their marriage could be a Christian unity. In God's eyes, this was far more important than whether or not they purchased a Mercedes. If the matter had been a black-and-white issue, such as cheating on income taxes, that would have been different, but buying a Mercedes fell in the gray area. Submission involves faith, faith that God sees and will bless: whether that is changing your husband's heart or bringing good out of the decision. We must, as Jesus did, commit our case to the One who judges justly.

When Point of Grace received a Dove Award for being the group of the year in 1999, they gave thanks to their husbands for allowing them to be involved in a ministry that had them on the road so much. I'm sure some women watching felt sick to their stomachs. Yet the women of Point of Grace have marriages that are a Christian unity. Together they and their husbands seek God's face and submit to one another. What a glorious heritage of harmony to pass on to their children!

HARMONY IN THE BODY OF CHRIST

The same principle of learning how to submit to one another in marriage applies to every close relationship. Though you are *sexually* one only with a spouse, God is pleased when we can become *emotionally* and *spiritually* one with close friends, business partners, and brothers and sisters in the body of Christ. It means listening, praying, and submitting.

The writing of *My Daughter, My Daughter* has repeatedly exemplified this. When Sandi Patty first saw my chapter concerning her, she was understandably uncomfortable. *Couldn't Dee just talk around my fall?* she thought. However, submissively, she read the chapter to her accountability group, and they encouraged her to allow it to be published. They said, "This is the truth, and the truth will take you into a deeper walk with God." Her pastor told her the same thing. So then Sandi submitted herself to God, who spoke to her. Sandi told me: "God put in my heart: 'Sandi, I am the God of truth and where there is truth, I am there. So trust Me.'" The result? An overwhelming peace and harmony—and freedom!

On the video for *My Daughter, My Daughter* Sandi tells how she has learned so much about God's grace in the last few years, and then she sings, as only Sandi can, of how He has set her free. If you have an opportunity to hear Sandi today, I believe you will sense a deeper anointing on her, an anointing that followed her submission to Him and the body of Christ.

Likewise, because Lori and I have worked together on this book, we have had to submit to each other. I am doing the writing, and Lori has provided access for interviews with the Heritage Keepers team, speakers, and singers. Together Lori and I have prayed about the title, the cover, and the content. It is a joy not to be alone in this, for two are better than one, but it can also be a problem. What do we do when we disagree? We pray, we seek God, and we have asked my e-mail prayer team to do the same. We submit our ideas and ourselves to one another, and also to the Chariot Victor Publishing team. It is a challenge, but I believe it also serves God's deeper purpose of helping us, in the body of Christ, to become one. When brainstorming about the title, we must have gone through fifty titles. Again and again we cried out to God: "Lord, please—we don't want our idea, we want Your idea!" One day when I was praying through the Heritage Keepers' psalm, Psalm 78, I read the opening again, God's plaintive cry to His people:

Oh my people, hear my teaching....

Suddenly I saw the tenderness, the emotion, and I sensed God reaching out to me, saying:

My daughter, My daughter
My precious child ...

I felt a quickening in my spirit. Was this it? I showed it to my assistant, Gay, who had not been terribly enthusiastic about any of our titles.

"Yes!" she said.

"Yes?" I said, excitedly.

"Yes. It reminds me of my identity. It makes me feel loved. Yes."

Immediately I faxed the title to Lori in Wichita. Minutes later the phone rang. Lori was talking so quickly I had to listen intently to catch all her words:

"I have goosebumps. Oh, Dee, this is so amazing. Last night when we were coming home from a game, some of the kids from our team in the car in front of us had an accident."

"What happened?" I asked.

"It was black as could be and two horses wandered out on the road. They hit them."

I gasped. "Oh, no."

"It's okay, it's okay. They are okay," she assured me. "But it was very very scary. The thud—the screech—and we didn't know what was happening. With racing hearts we jumped out—and, thank God, they were all okay, though really shaken up. This morning when I took my kids to school I thought about how much I loved them, and how dear they were to me, and how devastated I'd be if anything happened to them. I was thinking, "My son, my son. My daughter, my daughter.""

"Wow," I said, now understanding why she was telling me all this.

"That's not all, Dee." Lori continued, breathlessly: "We have a mischievous yellow Lab named Tanner. When we were pulling out of our drive to go to school, Daniel said, "Look Mom! Doesn't Tanner look sooo precious." Precious is not a word I expected to hear from a fourteen-year-old boy, so it stuck in my mind. I wondered if he would one day call his wife *precious*. So, on the way home I'm thinking, *My son, my son. My daughter, my daughter. Precious.* Then I walk into the office, see that there is a fax, pick it up, and read:

My Daughter, My Daughter
My precious child ...

"Wow," I said, again.

Of course then we had to submit our idea to the people at Chariot Victor Publishing. Understandably, they raised their eyebrows at our process for it was not their usual process. Again, more listening, more prayer, and more submission to one another. At one point, when Lori and I were becoming frustrated and angry, one of the editors restored our perspective by gently saying: "We must not be adversaries, we are a team." Psalm 133:1 says:

Behold, how good and how pleasant it is for brethren to dwell together in
unity! (KJV)

How can we dwell together in unity? By seeking God and submitting to one another. More important than this book is our harmonious relationship in the body of Christ. The Enemy would love to see us divided in our homes, in our churches, and in the body of Christ—but God longs for us to be one. That is our heritage.

REVERSING OTHER EFFECTS OF THE FALL

There are additional effects of the Fall that can be reversed through the power of Christ. Men and women would each suffer in an area that before was only a blessing to them. Work, a good gift from God (present before the Fall), would now have trials and frustrations. (Wouldn't it be great to garden without weeds?) Children, a good gift from God (intended before the Fall), would now come forth in painful labor. (Wouldn't it be great to have children without pain?) My friend Bev Lowry (who is the mother of comedian Mark Lowry) told me she thinks the effect for women goes beyond childbirth to all the suffering that mothering encompasses. I don't know whether she is right or not (and certainly being Mark's mother had to be a challenge), but it is an intriguing thought. There is so much joy in mothering, but there is, definitely, pain as well.

Commentator G. von Rad observes: "The woman's punishment struck at the deepest root of her being a wife and mother; the man's punishment strikes at the innermost nerve of his life: his work, his activity, and provision for sustenance."[1]

God's grace can help us to have the strength to face the effects of the Fall, whether it is the pain of childbirth, the weeds in our work world, or the last enemy: death. Because of sin every man and every woman is destined to die. Romans 6:23a says: "The wages of sin is death." Those of us who have seen a loved one through the icy waters of death know that death, indeed, is an enemy—but the last enemy, for if you have put your trust in Christ, He is waiting at the other side.

There is a striking scene in John Bunyan's *Pilgrim's Progress* where

Christian and Hopeful come to the icy waters of death. On the other side is the Celestial City, but the deep, dark river separates them. They look to the left, and they look to the right. But the men on the bank say:

You have to go through it. There is no bridge.

HARMONY WITH GOD

Christ has made it possible to reverse the final effect of the Fall, which is death. Romans 6:23 says: "For the wages of sin is death, but the gift of God is eternal life in Christ Jesus our Lord." Do you know *how* to have victory over the last enemy? Do you have the absolute assurance that you are headed to heaven, to the "Celestial City"? If you have doubt, God longs to wipe that doubt away. In the Bible study you will learn how to have confidence that you have eternal life.

Then, we will continue on with our story. I am eager to tell you the poignant way God revealed the name, Heritage Keepers.

Panning for Heritage Gold

☀ Icebreaker: Finish *one* of the following sentences:

A. The hardest thing for me in childbirth is …

B. The hardest thing for me in facing death is …

1. What stood out to you from the text and Scriptures in the fourth chapter? Why?

Review Genesis 4:6-7.

2. The word "desires" is the Hebrew word *shuquah*. How is it used here?

As an overview, read Genesis 3:14-19.

3. Why do you think God interrogates Adam and Eve, but not the serpent?

Read Genesis 3:14-15.

4. What is prophesied in Genesis 3:15?

Many see in the above verse, in addition to a long struggle between man and Satan, the first promise—the promise of the Cross and its victory in crushing Satan's head.

☀ 5. Read slowly the poetry of Genesis 2:22-24. Write down all the observations you can discover. What do you see?

6. What does it mean to you that "the two shall be one flesh"?

7. Why is God opposed to divorce? (Malachi 2:13-16; Matthew 19:4-6)

If you have been hurt by divorce, either personally or through your parents, describe some of the pain of divorce.

8. Why is God opposed to sex outside of marriage? (1 Corinthians 6:16)

If you have been hurt by sex outside of marriage, either personally or through your parents, describe some of the pain of sexual promiscuity.

Read Genesis 3:16.

9. What are some of the consequences of the Fall for the woman?

Do you think "desire" in verse 16 refers to the "desire to dominate" or to "sexual desire?" Explain your reasoning.

10. Think of a time when you and your husband (or you and a close friend or relative) were each desiring your own way. Describe your feelings at that time.

Think of time when you and your husband (or you and a close friend or relative) submitted to one another out of reverence for Christ. Describe your feelings at that time.

Read Ephesians 5:21-33.

11. What command is given to all believers?

What command is given to wives?

What command is given to husbands?

12. Describe how the above commands can help overcome the effects of the fall and restore harmony.

☀ Read Genesis 3:17-19.

13. What are some of the consequences of the Fall for the man?

14. Why do you think God's judgment was, for Eve, in the area of being a wife and mother, and for Adam, in the area of being a provider?

Read 1 Corinthians 15:22-28.

15. What inheritance do we have from Adam (v. 22a) What inheritance can we have in Christ? (22b)

Who is the last enemy? (26)

Read 1 Corinthians 15:35-58.

16. How will our resurrected body be different from our earthly body? (v. 40-44)

17. Who reverses the effects of the Fall? (v. 45b; v. 57)

18. How did Christ pay for our sins? (See 1 Peter 2:24-25)

In addition to pardoning us, *why* did Christ die for us? (1 Peter 2:24)

Read 1 John 5:13.

19. Why does John write these things? Does he say "hope" or "know"?

20. Some Christians are dominated by sin; others are dominated by the Spirit. What secret can you discover for victorious living from Romans 8:5?

21. What has God shown you through this lesson? Is He whispering to you in any way?

Next week would be a great time to schedule a luncheon or pajama party.

Prayer Time:

Pair off in twos or threes and pray conversationally concerning your answer to question 21. Then pray conversationally concerning other needs in your life.

Five

Women from three generations gathered around the table: aunts, cousins, Lori, me—just as we had when Grandma was alive. We were pouring over our Bibles when someone ran and got Grandma's Bible. When we opened it, there was her white crocheted cross and prayers, with our names, filling the margins. Emotion swept over us as we each reminisced about Grandma. I remembered how she stood by me during the hardest time in my life. Somebody else remembered her in the hospital, and how she was praying for the children yet to be born. And then a holy hush came over the kitchen. Suddenly, we knew what this woman's conference was supposed to be about.

KIM JONES, LORI'S SISTER

We Need to Be Heritage Keepers!

*N*ow that Lori and Bob's hearts were yielded, closed doors mysteriously swung open, one after another.

The first Heritage Keepers conference was to be held in the generous sanctuary of Wichita Central Community Church on August 10, 1996—less than seven months away. The problem? Well-known speakers are booked at least a year in advance.

Driving to work at Central Community that final week in January, Bob was listening to "Focus on the Family." Marge Caldwell was the guest and captivated him. Bob reached for his cell phone: "Lori—turn on your radio! Oh, Lori—just listen to her! We've got to call her."

And then, in a pattern that was to become almost comical, they discovered Marge was booked. A few days later, Marge called back. She'd had a cancellation—would they still like her to come on August 10?

A man named Lou Lutz (Lefty) who was delivering Susi Cakes to the church stuck his head in Bob's office: "I hear you are going to do a women's style Promise Keepers. What would you think about John Trent being a speaker?"

Bob had been blessed by John's speaking at Promise Keepers. *Of course we'd love John Trent*, Bob thought, *but how?* Lefty continued, "John is a friend of mine. I think he might be interested in this." Bob and Lori called John and found he was booked. Within a week John's office called back and said he'd had a cancellation. Would they still like John Trent on August 10?

When this happened yet again with another well-known speaker, Lori said, "We just giggled because it was so clear that it wasn't our plan, but that God was in charge." God was going before them, opening the sea. Within ten days they had all their speakers and musicians.

Everything seemed to be coming together. What *was* missing was a name. What should this women's conference be called?

The story I am going to tell you gives us a glimpse into the mysterious workings of God. God had a plan for this women's conference, but He didn't reveal it all at once. Rather, as He often seems to do, He gave those whom He called enough light to take a few steps, and then He gave them more light for another few steps. As time progressed, the path became clearer and clearer, and the purpose for Heritage Keepers more defined. As Lori and Bob turned around and looked back on the winding path, they stood in awe of His plan from beginning to end.

THE FIRST GLIMPSE OF THE NAME: JUNE 1994

Eighteen months before the call to Bob and Lori, God had planted the seed for the word *heritage* in the mind of one of Lori's dearest friends, Cindy Baldwin. Before I tell you this story, it will be helpful to understand something of the depth of the word *heritage*.

The scriptural word *heritage* is one of those concepts with incredible profundity. Just when you think you have plumbed the depths, you realize it was a false bottom, and your scope sinks deeper. I believe this next truth will minister to you deeply. It makes me feel cherished, wrapped in the blanket of God's protective love.

Not only can we look back to a godly heritage through our holy ancestors like Abraham and Sarah, but we *are*, if we have put our trust in Christ, God's heritage. God chose a people for His own, and that was Israel, and later, all who would put their trust in Christ, Jews *and* Gentiles. Those who have faith become the children of Abraham, part of God's heritage. This people is God's peculiar people, His chosen generation, His *heritage*. Like golden links in a chain: Abraham and Sarah, Isaac and Rebekah, Jacob and Rachel, and on into the twenty-first century—God has a people who are His heritage. You can see God's anger against those who have harmed His heritage, the anger of a father as when his precious daughter has been violated. Feel God's emotion in the Book of Joel. The invading nations have violated the apple of God's eye, His heritage.

> *I will judge them for harming my people* [KJV says: my heritage]. …
> *They cast lots to decide which of my people would be their slaves. They traded young boys for prostitutes and little girls for enough wine to get drunk.*
> *…The sun and the moon will grow dark, and the stars will no longer shine. The Lord's voice will roar from Zion and thunder from Jerusalem, and the earth and heavens will begin to shake. But to his people of Israel* [His heritage]*, the Lord will be a welcoming refuge and a strong fortress.* (Joel 3:2-3; 15-16 NLT)

Think of the rage you feel when another hurts someone who is precious to you. I remember picking up our then ten-year-old son at a Seattle public swimming pool. Johnny's shoulders were shaking; his face was tear streaked; and his beach towel, shirt, and Nikes were missing. He told me some teenage bullies had taken them. He also told me they had held him under water.

HELD YOU UNDER WATER? Rage welled up in me. ***WHERE ARE THEY?*** When his eyes lifted in the direction of some big boys who were snickering at him, I charged toward them, like a lioness protecting her cub, and ripped into them verbally. If I had had the power to darken the sun and moon and shake the heavens to teach those bullies a lesson, I would have!

God *has* that power, and He loves us, His heritage, far more fiercely than even a mother can love her baby. When Israel said, *"The Lord has forsaken me, the Lord has forgotten me"* (Isaiah 49:14), God cried in response:

> *"Can a mother forget the baby at her breast and have no compassion on the child she has borne?*
> *Though she may forget, I will not forget you!*
> *See, I have engraved you on the palms of my hands."* (Isaiah 49:15)

God communicated this concept to Lori's dear friend Cindy Baldwin in 1994, showing, as Lori is quick to say, that this is not "a Lori story, but a God story." Lori is just one of a line of vessels God called, whispering,

> *O my precious child*
> *incline your ear*

Cindy is one of those indispensable behind-the-scenes workers at Heritage Keepers. It was Cindy who made three trips to the airport for me when my plane was delayed three times because of summer storms. Ever cheerful, ever encouraging, her vivacious spirit boosts us all. It was Cindy who hugged my weak-kneed daughter Sally after Sally had gotten a glimpse of the crowd in the arena and promised her, "I'll be praying for you *every second* you are up there!" Over a year before God called Lori, God spoke to Cindy. Cindy told me:

I remember the morning. I was completely devastated. Our only two children, teenagers, were spinning out of control—particularly, our son Matt. One morning I had just had it. I was in my bedroom and I fell on the floor, sobbing and pounding my fists on the carpet. I said: "Lord, I can't do it anymore. I don't want to do it anymore. You have to take this from me. I have no more strength." Then, though not audibly, yet in a strong voice I knew was not my own, I heard:

"You are My heritage. You are My future. Matt is My child. You have to let go."

God had not forgotten Cindy. God had not forgotten Matt. He was in control. They were *His heritage, His treasured possession.* Cindy could trust God to take care of Matt because Matt belonged to God. She, and Matt, and each son and daughter of Abraham are God's future, His holy heritage. We are the link in the chain for future generations, and we are of great value to God.

The same emotional cry that comes through the prophets comes through Peter, when he writes to us, as the children of Abraham:

But you are a chosen people, a royal priesthood, a holy nation, a people belonging to God, that you may declare the praises of him who called you out of darkness into his wonderful light. Once you were not a people, but now you are the people of God; once you had not received mercy, but now you have received mercy. (1 Peter 2:9-10)

THE CORK AND CANAPÉ CAFE: FALL 1995

On an Indian summer day in 1995, Cindy and Lori lingered over hazelnut coffees at the *Cork and Canapé Cafe* in Wichita. It had been more than a year since God had spoken to Cindy, assuring her that her son Matt was *His heritage.* Cindy shared soul to soul with Lori, as good women friends are apt to do, telling Lori how God had spoken to her. Cindy's eyes filled at the memory, and at the way she had seen God at work in Matt's life in the ensuing year. Before they parted Lori embraced Cindy, and then she drove home, turning this precious truth over and over in her mind, warmed by its reassuring message. *We belong to God. We are His heritage. We are loved with an everlasting love.*

It was just a seed. Just one word: *heritage.* In December of 1995, Lori would receive the call to do "a women's style Promise Keepers." The word heritage had not yet pushed its head through the surface. That green leaf would appear, appropriately, the following Saint Patrick's Day.

WINFIELD, KANSAS: MARCH 17, 1996

Do you remember how Dorothy, at the close of *The Wizard of Oz,* clicks her heels together, closes her eyes, and says: "There's no place like home! There's no place like home!"? Then she and Toto are whisked back to home sweet home—the farmhouse in Kansas with Auntie Em, a white picket fence, snowy lace curtains fluttering in the breeze, and corn on the cob. That picturesque Kansas scene is pretty close to the environment in which Lori grew up.

Lori doesn't have an Auntie Em, but she does have four aunts (one is Dorothy!) and an uncle who grew up in the little town of Winfield, Kansas. Lori's family lived just a block from her grandmother, and another block from aunts and uncles. On Sundays they all gathered together at Grandma's house. When Lori describes those Sunday afternoons I envision the warm golden scenes of a Norman Rockwell painting: the men are gathered around a game on TV in the family room, the women are knitting and laughing around a large oak kitchen table, and the children are playing softball in the backyard. "I can't really express in words," Lori said, "what it meant to grow up with that kind of extended family love and support. It wasn't just Sundays that we were together, any excuse would do: birthdays, anniversaries, a ball game. My cousin Shelly was like a sister to me—that's how close knit our family was. And if somebody had a dream, they were listened to with hearing ears, they were supported with prayer, and they were spoiled rotten with love."

If you were to come behind the scenes at a Heritage Keepers conference you would see the message being delivered onstage lived out offstage. Like an army of ants carrying a four-tiered cake, three generations of the Beckler and Bowling families pull together and host these megaconferences. Grandparents answer the phone, aunts and uncles stuff envelopes, siblings and cousins huddle in prayer, and children serve coffee and sandwiches. How appropriate God revealed the name *Heritage Keepers* at a family gathering in Winfield, Kansas.

Bob and Lori returned to Winfield on Saint Patrick's Day Sunday to sing a duet in Lori's childhood church. Afterward they gathered at Aunt Louise's home for Sunday dinner and a family reunion. Even Aunt Dorothy was visiting from New Mexico. Waves of nostalgia washed over them. Lori said, "It felt like we were at Grandma's again, the way we had gathered each Sunday when I was a child."

As the women were catching up on one another's lives, Lori mentioned the women's conference. Immediately it caught their attention and each woman became excited, buzzing with questions. Lori said the conference was still nameless, and the women immediately started brainstorming: Promise Reapers—Daughters of the King. It intrigues me to see that at this point they still didn't have the clear vision that this conference would be about passing on the heritage. The thought was still primarily around "a women's style Promise Keepers." They prayed: *Lord, what is your message? What do you want?*

Around the table were six different denominations: Lutheran, Baptist, Methodist, Nazarene, Evangelical Free, and Christian. From one denomination they had branched into six, yet, they were still one in Christ. As they held hands around the table and bowed their heads, asking God for His name, they had a wonderful sense of unity. When they lifted their heads, Aunt Louise marveled: "We have such a rich heritage."

Cousin Shelly remembers that suddenly there was a silence, as they considered Louise's comment. "That, I think," she said, "was the moment of revelation." Finally, Lori said, "Yes! This is about our heritage." Her mind flashed back to her lunch with Cindy Baldwin, and the understanding that we are God's heritage. Excitedly, everybody began flipping through their Bibles, looking in their concordances. Again, they laughed at their diversity, for together they had five different translations of the Bible. Aunt Ramona said, "We should have Grandma's *King James Version* here too—I'll run home and get it."

Lori's sister Kim said, "When we opened Grandma's Bible we became very emotional. It was like she was at the table with us. There, in her highlighted Bible, in her small script in the margins, were prayers with *our names,* prayers we had no idea she prayed. A holy hush fell over us as we realized what an incredible legacy, what an incredible *heritage* had been passed down to us. And we were all reminded, through Grandma's example, of what a responsibility we had: as grandmothers, as moms, as aunts—to pass on that heritage to the next generation."

They reminisced about the last days of Grandma's life in the hospital. Shelly said, "Even though she couldn't talk because there were tubes down her nose and throat, she was scribbling notes, thinking about her children, her grandchildren, and the children yet to be born. She was thinking about the generations to come, and praying they would have faith. And here we were, the answer to her prayers."

Now and then God gives us a "Precious Pause" in our life, a golden moment that you wish would stay, but which flits away like an elusive butterfly, and yet, changes you forever. That afternoon was one of those "Precious Pauses." As the women listened to Grandma's prayers read aloud, they realized anew that they belonged to a God who bends down and answers prayer. And though Grandma was no longer on earth, she had been a strong link in the chain. They also had the sense God was bending down to them that afternoon, asking them to be a strong link in the chain, and encouraging other women to be. Excitedly they poured over Grandma's Bible with a sense of expectancy, aware of the presence of a holy God. One of the aunts (no one can remember which one!) turned to Psalm 78, and said, "Oh my. Look at Psalm 78!" Together they turned to it. Aunt Ramona read the opening seven verses from Grandma Bowling's *King James Bible*, closing with:

> *That the generation to come might know them, even the children which should be born; who should arise and declare them to their children: That they might set their hope in God, and not forget the works of God, but keep his commandments.*

Lori said, "I still remember the moment. We were so into this, so absorbed: I can still picture the expressions on their faces. And one of my aunts, I can't even remember which one, was cutting the cake. With the knife poised in midair, she said, 'we need to keep God's heritage—we need to be heritage keepers.' We were quiet, and then we laughed. It all sounded kind of hokey, and we were all so emotional. We'd been doing this for four hours. But then, it was like, 'Yes! We've got to be Heritage Keepers.'"

That truth was confirmed as they read on in Psalm 78, which describes God's heartache because *His children, His heritage*, had forgotten their past. The very children of the fathers and mothers who had walked through the Red Sea had forgotten. Aunt Ramona kept reading:

> *They forgot his deeds and his wonders that he had shown them....*
> *He split the sea and brought them through it,*
> *and caused the water to stand up like a wall*
> *And then he led them with a cloud by day*
> *and all night by a fiery light....*
> *But they continued to sin against him....*
> *And they spoke against God, saying,*
> *"Is God able to prepare a table in the wilderness?*
> *True, he struck a rock, and water gushed out and streams flowed—*
> *But can he also provide bread?*
> *Can he supply meat for his people?"*
> (Excerpts from Psalm 78:11-20 *Word Biblical Commentary Translation*)

"Yes," Shelly said, "we need to be Heritage Keepers."

HERITAGE KEEPERS

If you were blessed with a godly family as the Becklers and Bowlings have been, you need to pass it on, you need to be a strong link in the chain. If you are not blessed with that kind of heritage, then you can be the first link. You can start recording the ways God has worked in your life, and this book will be laced with ideas. Here are a few to get you started:

Like Grandma Bowling did, pray. Pray for your children, your grandchildren, and the children yet to be born. Write their names in the margins when you are praying through a verse for them.

Tell stories: tell your children and your grandchildren how God has worked in your life.

Keep records. My daughter-in-law, Julie, makes beautiful photo albums with pictures and stories telling of answered prayers. She has one large album called Against Forgetting, full of answers to prayers. When their daughter, Emily, was three, she prayed for a brother, so of course a whole page is dedicated to pictures of Simeon and his big sister's prayers. These albums are an inheritance more precious than silver.

*Act out stories. Children absolutely adore acting out the dramatic stories from the Bible: the parting of the Red Sea, David and Goliath, the raising of Lazarus, etc. We acted our way through the Bible when our children were little. (We've done that with international students as well—it crosses the language barrier.) A favorite is Jesus stopping the storm. We hop on a towel, which is our boat, and let the children wave a blue sheet, making a stormy sea. We cry—we yell for help! And then Jesus, played by a child, stands up, extends his arms, and says, "Peace, be still." Our eyes grow big. We say, "**WHO IS THIS? EVEN THE WIND AND WAVES OBEY HIM!**" Will they forget? They haven't. Instead, they are doing dramatizations now with their children. The holy heritage we are studying in this book (stories of Sarah, Jacob, Miriam, and others) has been divided into simple skits in Appendix B. Child Evangelism Fellowship says:*

Children forget what they hear.
Children understand what they see.
Children remember what they do.

Understanding is key to remembering. Charles Spurgeon says that the reason the Israelites forgot the miracles was because they didn't understand, and "what is not understood will soon be forgotten." Though they saw the miraculous plagues, though they saw the Red Sea divide, they "ignorantly wondered at them," but failed to understand "their design of love, their deep moral and spiritual lessons, and their revelation of divine power and justice." This should be a lesson to us as mothers or mentors. We must help the next generation understand, and we can do that through skits, through discussions, and through talking about how to apply what we learned to our lives today. We need to be heritage keepers.

As women, we particularly need to look back to the holy women of the past. That is what Peter tells us to do in 1 Peter 3. In fact, he tells us we can be Sarah's daughters if we do what is right and don't give way to hysterical fears. (1 Peter 3:6)

Do you know what that means? It's fascinating. We will look at this carefully. But first, do the Bible study, because it contains the call of God to you through Psalm 78.

Panning for Heritage Gold

If you are doing this study at a longer session, such as a pajama party, the questions that have you recalling God's power in your own life can be answered more extensively.

☀ Icebreaker: In one breath share one time when God's presence or power was very real to you.

1. What stood out to you from the text and Scriptures in the fifth chapter? Why?

2. What does it mean to you that you *are* God's heritage?

Read Psalm 78 as an overview.

3. What emotions did you sense? (Give verses.)

What repeated theme did you see? (Give verses.)

What phrases stood out to you? (Give verses.)

☼ Read Psalm 78:1-8.

4. These opening verses establish the intention of the psalmist. What is it?

Read Psalm 78:9-20.

Often Scripture will refer to a whole group of people by the name of a famous ancestor. "Ephraim" probably represents the whole Northern tribe and the miracles they witnessed over time are merged together in this section.

5. List some of the miracles God did for the Israelites.

Yet, what was their response? (vv. 19-20)

6. What are some ways God has bent down and ministered to you in your life? List a few ways.

How can you avoid repeating the sins of your ancestors?

Read Numbers 11.

7. Describe the complaint of the people. (vv. 4-6) How does God respond? (vv. 18-20 and v. 33)

"Egypt" is a picture of slavery, of bondage to sin. What had God's people forgotten about Egypt?

Why does God sometimes give us over to our lusts?

Read Psalm 78:21-31.

8. How can you see the grace of God and the judgment of God together in these passages?

The next time you are discontented, how can you learn from the above story so that you do not repeat the sin of your ancestors?

Read Psalm 78:32-39.

9. Describe the mercy of God. Describe the problem of God's people.

☀ Read Psalm 78:40-72.

10. How did God fight for His people, His heritage, in Egypt? (vv. 43-53)

How did they respond? (vv. 40-42)

11. How did God fight for them after they had left Egypt? (v. 55)

How did they respond? (vv. 56-58)

How did God respond to their unfaithfulness? (vv. 59-64)

What does He call them? (v. 62b)

What does God then do for His inheritance, His heritage? (vv. 65-72) (This word is the same word used in Joel 3 where God was angry at the nations who had hurt His people, His inheritance.)

12. When the psalm opened, it spoke of riddles from the past. What riddle do you see being repeated through the story? (Answer on your own before you look ahead.)

13. How have you failed the Lord in major ways?

14. What hope does this psalm give you?

The riddle is God's saving work on behalf of His heritage despite their disgraceful behavior. We can identify, for God has been so good to us as well, yet we have forgotten and failed Him, giving in to the power of sin. But because we are His heritage, He doesn't abandon us forever. Kidner writes of? "a grace that persists through all the judgments."[2]

15. What are you doing to pass on the mighty acts of God in history and in your own life to the next generation? Be specific.

Charles H. Spurgeon writes, in response to Psalm 78: *Around the fireside fathers* [and mothers] *should repeat not only the Bible records, but the deeds of the martyrs and reformers, and moreover the dealings of the Lord with themselves both in providence and grace.*[3] See Appendix C for a list of books.

Read Isaiah 49:15 and give thanks to God.

Prayer Time:

Have a time of praise and thanksgiving for the mighty acts of God: include those from Scripture and those from your own life.

Six

*You are her daughter if you do what is right
and do not give way to fear.*

1 PETER 3:6

Daughters
of Sarah

*A*fter speaking at a prayer breakfast in Fargo, North Dakota, I had lunch with the committee of twelve women. Their speaker the previous year had been Anne Graham Lotz, and she had recently called this committee, asking them, though her ministry could not offer financial backing, to pray about hosting a crusade for women in Fargo. The committee had to make a decision soon. Was God leading them to step out on faith and rent the Fargo Dome?

To encourage them, I told them the story of Heritage Keepers, and of how God led a couple with very little money to rent large arenas for the conferences. "God has blessed it," I said, "because it was His plan, which is what you need to discern. If it is His plan, that doesn't mean there won't be frightening times, but God will come through for you."

One of the women asked, "Did the money they needed come in?"

I paused. "In the beginning they ran ahead of God. After thousands came to the first event, a few hundred came to another, despite the fact they had rented a large arena and brought in big-name speakers. They nearly lost their house and their parents' retirement savings." (That story is in the next chapter.) A hush came over the table as the women exchanged fearful glances.

"What on earth did they do?" one woman finally asked.

"They didn't give way to hysterical fears. They prayed, trusted, and God came through, in His time."

Whatever God calls you to, He wants you to "do what is right and not give way to hysterical fears." He wants us to be against forgetting His power and His mighty acts, to trust Him, and not give way to fear. This is how Peter says we become "a daughter of Sarah."

HOPING IN GOD IN THE FACE OF HUGE PROBLEMS

One of my favorite Heritage Keepers moments occurred when Bobbie and Kenny McCaughey, parents of the septuplets, visited the Wichita conference in 1999. The famous parents sat on a sofa on stage, holding hands, as Bob and Lori interviewed them. Bobbie, tears flowing freely, shared how she felt the day the ultrasound revealed she was carrying seven babies.

"We had wanted one baby." [Audience laughs] "The doctors were standing in front of the screen counting: 'One, two, three, four, five, six, seven.' I said, 'You're not counting babies, are you?'"

Bob Beckler asked Kenny: "How did you feel when she told you how many babies there was going to be?"

"I was like, WHOA! I went straight to the back bedroom and just paced. I probably paced the floor of that little house a hundred times that day, saying, *Lord, why? What's going on here? What are You doing here?*"

Yet Kenny and Bobbie, from the very beginning, set their hope in God. And God gave them a peace. Kenny said, "We had a feeling deep within our hearts that we were going to have seven healthy babies— and that this could only come from God. We knew that since this was such a God-sized problem [laughter], that's the wrong word—blessing! I said that because that's how the world views it . . . but when God gives you a problem that's so big and huge that you say, *Lord, I don't know if I can do this,* God turns right back around and says, *Yes, you can. You let Me do it.*"

Bobbie told of miracle after miracle, which amazed the medical community. "Throughout the entire pregnancy, compared to other multiple pregnancies I've heard about, we had a walk in the park. I had very few difficulties. But the ones that we did have were major scares and I would think: *Lord, what are You doing? You gave us the seven babies, we've accepted them, and now after all this You're going to take them away.* But it was just more testing. I felt like God was seeing what we were going to do with what He had given us and how we were going to handle it. And each time, everything was okay." At one point it looked as if they were going to lose "Baby D" because she didn't have enough amniotic fluid. They, their family, and brothers and sisters in Christ they had never met prayed. The next morning "Baby D's" amniotic fluid had doubled. "God took care of the babies," Bobbie told the audience.

Peter tells us we become daughters of Sarah by putting our hope in God and not giving way to hysterical fears. Bobbie is a true daughter of Sarah.

HOPING IN GOD IN THE FACE OF DEATH

Putting your hope in God doesn't guarantee you a smooth road, but, instead, that God will do all things well in His time. When a crazed teenager put his gun to the head of seventeen-year-old Cassie Bernall at Columbine High School in Littleton, Colorado and asked her if she believed in God, she hesitated. I'm sure she was counting the cost. In the third chapter of 1 Peter, Peter quotes from Isaiah, saying "Do not fear what they fear." What does the world fear? Man. Cassie chose not to fear man and said, "Yes, I believe." The gunman shot her and she became a teenage martyr. Many came to faith at her funeral, and many believers have been strengthened because of Cassie to live wholeheartedly for Christ. Tertullian wrote: "The blood of the martyrs is indeed the seed of the church."[1] Cassie is a true daughter of Sarah.

What will you do if you are faced with a difficult pregnancy, marriage, or ministry? What if you cannot pay your bills? What if you are asked to deny your Lord? Will you choose an unholy path, or will you put your trust in God? God has given us Sarah as a model, and Peter points to her as he encourages Christians who were living in a time of extreme persecution.

THE SETTING: HUMAN TORCHES AND PERSECUTED WIVES

Peter's first letter was written to Christians undergoing savage persecution. When Rome was burned in the first century, the emperor, Nero, was blamed. Needing a scapegoat, Nero had Christians arrested, blaming them, and burning them as human torches as supposed retribution.[2] Imagine the feelings you would have had as a wife, mother, and woman. How easy it would have been way "to give way to hysterical fears."

In addition, many women who had put their trust in Christ were married to men who did not yet believe. In Peter's day, a woman was considered the property of her husband. A wife who became a Christian became "vulnerable to sharp criticism and harsh treatment" from her husband. It is in this setting of persecution and intimidation which Peter writes:

> *Wives, in the same way be submissive to your husbands so that, if any of them do not believe the word, they may be won over without words by the behavior of their wives, when they see the purity and reverence of your lives.* (1 Peter 3:1-2)

Some women, when they read the above instructions to wives, feel as though they've been kicked in the stomach and consequently come up fighting. However, I think they might not feel wounded and angry if, in addition to the setting of 1 Peter, they understood these verses in context.

CONTEXT, CONTEXT, CONTEXT

How often misunderstandings are a result of taking thoughts out of context. In June of '98, Promise Keepers was in Indianapolis. Our firstborn son, J.R., who lives in Indianapolis, called me during the Promise Keepers event. "Mom," he said, "you may be hassled when you come here to speak in two months with Heritage Keepers." He then explained that outside the stadium angry women from the feminist organization NOW (National Organization for Women) were marching with placards saying: **PROMISE KEEPERS UNFAIR TO WOMEN!**

Though these protesters had not heard the whole message, they were deeply offended by the soundbites they *had* heard: "The man is the head of the home" and "Be the spiritual leader in your home."

How important those seeking the truth hear the whole message. Likewise, when you take verses out of context, they can seem harsh. Peter is not singling out women to be submissive, but commanding *all* believers to have a spirit of humility and gentleness. Consider this pattern in 1 Peter, where, one by one, Peter tells believers to submit:

Peter tells citizens to submit to the government. (1 Peter 2:13) In being submissive they were being a good witness. They were not to be rabble-rousers.

*Peter tells slaves **in the same way** to submit to their masters.* (1 Peter 2:18) Though slavery was wrong, the slaves were not to revolt, but to trust God to be their advocate.

Peter shows how Christ submitted to an unjust death. (1 Peter 2:21-23) Jesus did not retaliate but committed himself to God, who judges justly.

After these three examples,

*Peter tells wives "**in the same way** be submissive to your husbands so that, if any of them do not believe the word, they may be won over without words by the behavior of their wives."* (1 Peter 3:1)

When you see Peter's command to wives in context, suddenly it doesn't seem unfair. The pattern (which so often helps us to understand the truths of Scripture) is that God honors a servant spirit and uses it to advance the Gospel.

HOW TO MELT INSTEAD OF HARDEN A HEART

What does not advance the Gospel? A chip on our shoulder. Arguments. Violence. Paul expresses this in 2 Timothy 2:24-26:

And the Lord's servant must not quarrel; instead, he must be kind to everyone, able to teach, not resentful. Those who oppose him he must gently instruct, in the hope that God will grant them repentance leading them to a knowledge of the truth, and that they will come to their senses and escape from the trap of the devil, who has taken them captive to do his will.

It is the way of Christ to persuade peaceably. Harriet Beecher Stowe demonstrated this powerfully when she wrote *Uncle Tom's Cabin*, a novel that sold four million copies and made a significant contribution to the ending of slavery in America. "Uncle Tom" put his trust in God when kicked, whipped, and separated from his family. The gentle and quiet witness of these slaves brought conviction to many white slaveowners. Though Stowe used stereotypes, still, many believing slaves did, indeed, submit and put their trust in God, clinging to the words of 1 Peter. *Uncle Tom's Cabin* changed hearts as Harriet Beecher Stowe gave a voice to the slaves. People realized black people were human and that the life they were being deprived of was a great sin against a holy God.

Likewise, I believe God has anointed Kathy Troccoli to change hearts toward the unborn. When she sings "A Baby's Prayer" at women's conferences, the song from a baby in the womb to the mother who is contemplating aborting her, a holy hush comes over the crowd. Kathy's dear friend Allyson Baker said:

"A Baby's Prayer" is one of the songs that people will remember the first time they hear it. It absolutely pierces your heart because the images are so clear. When I first heard it I was carrying a baby in my womb, and it touched me so deeply. It clearly gives a voice to the unborn.

Kathy, like Harriet Beecher Stowe, has proved herself to be a daughter of Sarah, doing what is right and not giving way to fear. And what a rippling impact! Senator Orin Hatch called Kathy and requested 535 videos of "A Baby's Prayer"—one for every member of the House and Senate.[3] Kathy said, "I have them ready!" Six months before, God had placed it on Kathy's heart to raise the money and make the videos. It's a gentle, beautiful video of little girls ballet dancing with

Kathy singing in the background. Kathy writes in her book *My Life Is in Your Hands:*

> With all the militancy around this volatile issue, I decided that a prayer from a baby's heart would extend a gentle mercy and forgiveness.[4]

The peaceable approach is not without teeth, for it is the way of Christ. Violence hardens hearts whereas a peaceable approach melts them. In chapter 9 I will tell you an incredible story of how seventy women spontaneously came forward, kneeling and sobbing, when Kathy sang "A Baby's Prayer" at a women's conference. The peaceable approach can change lives.

In the same way, a woman who puts her trust in God and has a gentle and quiet spirit is much more likely to win her husband to Christ than the woman who badgers him and becomes angry with him. Though she may feel like knocking him over the head with her Bible, it's not going to help! What works? Whether it is a husband, sister, or friend—we've got to love them into the Kingdom and let them catch a glimpse of the gentle Christ who lives within us.

Marge Caldwell, who has spoken regularly with Heritage Keepers, says, "My daddy was a profane man. When I begged mother to leave him when I was younger, she'd say, 'No darlin', God's gonna save him, and when He saves him, I want to be there to enjoy it.'" Marge's mother lived out the truth of 1 Peter. Her husband couldn't help but be drawn to a God who could fill his wife with gentleness and a confident hope. Marge's mother *did not forget* the power of God. If He could open the sea, He could open her husband's heart. Five years before he died he put his trust in his wife's God. Marge says, in her exuberant winsome way: "And they had five *fabulous* years." Marge's mother was a true daughter of Sarah, putting her hope in Christ and not giving way to hysterical fears.

COHEIRS, NOT DOORMATS

Do you realize how revolutionary it was for Peter to call wives "coheirs?" In a day when wives were regarded almost as slaves, Peter was saying they were equals, "coheirs in the gracious gift of life."

Women could not own property, in fact, they were considered property! It was considered inappropriate for a *woman* to sit at the feet of a rabbi. That's one of the reasons Martha may have been so upset with her sister Mary. Instead of sitting at Jesus' feet, Martha felt her sister belonged in the kitchen, helping her. Jesus was a revolutionary when He told Martha to let Mary stay. (Luke 10:38-42)

It intrigues me that centuries before, Abraham and Sarah seemed to understand that it was God's intention that they relate, not as master and slave, but as coheirs. Their marriage is a model of mutuality and respect. When Sarah had strong convictions about something, she expressed them to Abraham. Sarah was not a doormat, she was a coheir.

As the years passed, sin clouded our great heritage of being coheirs. Women were treated poorly, though the prophets raged against it. If a man tired of his wife, he cast her aside like used luggage and found a fresh new wife. In the book of Malachi the men are weeping because their prayers are being hindered. In Malachi 2:13-14, the prophet thunders:

> *You flood the Lord's altar with tears. You weep and wail because he no longer pays attention to your offerings or accepts them with pleasure from your hands. You ask, "Why?" It is because the Lord is acting as the witness between you and the wife of your youth, because you have broken faith with her, though **she is your partner**, the wife of your marriage covenant.*

How does God regard her? As a partner, a coheir!

Why Sarah?

When Peter tells women to look back at their holy heritage and study the models of the holy women of old, he specifically mentions Sarah. In 1 Peter 3:1-6, we read:

> *Wives, in the same way be submissive to your husbands so that, if any of*

them do not believe the word, they may be won over without words by the behavior of their wives, when they see the purity and reverence of your lives. Your beauty should not come from outward adornment, such as braided hair and the wearing of gold jewelry and fine clothes. Instead, it should be that of your inner self, the unfading beauty of a gentle and quiet spirit, which is of great worth in God's sight. For this is the way the holy women of the past who put their hope in God used to make themselves beautiful. They were submissive to their own husbands, like Sarah, who obeyed Abraham and called him her master. You are her daughters if you do what is right and do not give way to fear.

The introduction of Sarah into the passage broadens the scope from wives married to unbelievers to wives married to believers as well. Both are to put their hope in God and not give way to hysterical fears. Can being married to a believer be scary? You better believe it!

How do you think Sarah felt when Abraham said, "Pack up your robes, honey. We're leaving Haran. Kiss your family good-bye—because you will never see them again. God has called us to be sojourners on earth."

And how do you think she felt when, one morning, he took their only son Isaac up Mount Moriah? Did she know that Abraham intended, in obedience to God, to sacrifice Isaac? I don't know, but if she did, I am terribly impressed that she was not kicking and screaming and holding onto her men all the way up the mountain.

I am married to a strong Christian man, and I am so thankful to be. Yet there are times when he terrifies me. I remember the day he came to me and said, "I think we should adopt a child from an overseas orphanage." (Overseas orphanages teem with children who need homes.) "I think we are ready to meet one of their greatest needs. Let's take an older child, a handicapped child, or a sibling group. I think we should call Holt International Children's Services[5] and tell them to pray about it and give us whomever they feel led to give us."

How did I respond? I felt hysterical fear filling me and I said, as calmly as I could, "I don't think so."

But, in time, and through the counsel of godly friends, God changed my heart. We adopted Beth, a precious twelve year old from Thailand. And even though she is missing her left arm, she plays tennis, golf, and baseball. She even water-skis. Some of you have seen Beth's radiant smile at Heritage Keepers conferences. What a blessing she is. I am so thankful I didn't miss being Beth's mother. I *would* have had I not learned to follow in Sarah's steps and put my hope in God.

PETER IS NOT TELLING WIVES TO SUBMIT TO SIN

It is important to remember Sarah was not perfect. Like all mortals, she had feet of clay. Though she was a model of faith and integrity, there were times when even Sarah gave way to hysterical fears. She shouldn't, for example, have cooperated with Abraham when he showed *his* feet of clay and encouraged her to deceive the Pharaoh and say she was his (Abraham's) sister. Neither should she have taken things into her own hands and encouraged Abraham to father a child through Hagar. We have already seen that in these cases this couple stepped out of God's will. I am reviewing this because there are teachers who have interpreted 1 Peter 3 to say that wives should submit in all things, even sin. Yet if we come back to the principle of always looking at verses in context, we can see this is a false interpretation. If you read all of 1 Peter you will see the emphasis is on doing what is right. In fact, Peter repeats this again, in the following passage where he tells us to emulate our ancestor, Sarah. He says:

*You are her daughters **if you do what is right** and do not give way to fear.*

What should a woman do if her husband asks her to lie to his boss and say he is sick when he is really nursing a hangover? What should she do if he asks her to get an abortion? Or to watch a pornographic movie with him? It's simple, and it's right here in 1 Peter. ***She should do what is right and not give way to fear.*** It would be a terrible twisting of the Scriptures to say we should submit to any of these sins in order to win our husbands to Christ. A woman in this situation should gently say, "I love you, honey, but before God I cannot do that." If she keels into immorality, she is not going to impress him. The same is true with single women who are friends with non-Christian men. Wellington Boone honored his wife, Kathryn, before thousands at Heritage Keepers by telling how she had won him to the Lord before they were married:

> *I tried to kiss you. You wouldn't let me. You knew I wasn't saved. I want to tell you this now in front of all these people—I appreciate you for maintaining the standard then and maintaining it through our marriage. Small as you were and standing up to me. That boldness put inside of me a dedication.*

"That boldness put inside of me a dedication." Isn't that what Peter is saying? Set your hope in God! Don't worry about standing up to an unbelieving man—it may save his soul! Gently explain why you cannot date him. My friend Marilyn Pendleton said to a young man in college who was eager to date her: "I can't go out with you because I don't date boys who have not put their trust in Jesus Christ. But I would love it if you would come to the Bible study on campus." (He came, put his trust in Christ, and when he was mature, Marilyn dated and married him.)

Don't fret that your unbelieving husband may lose his temper when you gently take a stand against an immoral request—your calm confidence in God may save his soul! Don't go along with something you know to be absolutely wrong because of fear of a man. Later, when Peter elaborates on this passage he quotes from Isaiah, where God tells Isaiah that the *only* One Isaiah needs to fear is God Himself. It's a fascinating passage and we'll look at it in the Bible study.

The same principles apply to submission in other settings. We should submit to authority figures unless they ask us to sin. This is the model of Peter in Acts 4 when he and John were told to stop preaching Christ. Peter responded:

> *Judge for yourselves whether it is right in God's sight to obey you rather than God. For we cannot help speaking about what we have seen and heard. (Acts 4:19-20)*

Also if an employer asks us to sin, we should gently take a stand. A bookkeeper in a doctor's office told me: "For years I cooperated with the doctor in padding his expense account—writing down meals, hotels for tax purposes as business expenses when they were really personal expenses. I did it because I was afraid I would lose my job if I didn't. But I became increasingly convicted, so I prayed God would give me the faith to do what was right. The next time it happened, I told him, as gently as I could, that I was sorry I had not spoken up sooner, but that I was feeling uncomfortable turning in personal expenses as business expenses. I also told him I valued my job and I valued him. He stood there quietly. My heart was in my throat. Then he nodded, almost imperceptibly. He hasn't asked me to do it again, and at this point, I still have my job."

We become Sarah's daughters by **doing what is right and not giving way to fear.** That is not an excuse for being capricious in our submission. If a husband or a boss asks you to do something you do not want to do, but is not immoral, you may submit your opinion respectfully, but if he holds firm, God would have you submit with a gentle and quiet spirit. One executive secretary said, "It irritates me when my boss asks me to get her coffee. I have a master's degree—I don't like to be treated like a lackey." So often pride, and not godliness, is the reason we don't want to submit. Peter keeps pointing us back to Christ, who humbled himself again and again and again. Peter also points to Sarah's respectful attitude toward Abraham when she, in talking to herself, called him her "lord." (Genesis 18:12 KJV) In the same passage we see how eager she was to do Abraham's bidding. Three unexpected visitors came by their tent and Abraham said to her: "Quick, get three seahs [20 quarts!] of fine flour and knead it and bake some bread." Sarah did it cheerfully, and it turned out she was entertaining angels who had some very good news for her.

DON'T FLY AWAY LIKE A FRIGHTENED BIRD

Sarah shows real strength in the way she shares her heart with Abraham and we should do likewise. Jane Hansen, in *Fashioned for*

Intimacy, explains that this isn't always easy:

> As a woman begins to share her heart with her husband—even if she
> is gentle and kind—he may immediately become defensive and self-
> protective.[6]

Men, generally speaking, are not as comfortable as women in sharing heart to heart, in reciprocating to vulnerability with vulnerability. The Greek word Peter uses in 1 Peter 3:6 for *terror* (*don't be afraid with any terror*) is akin to a word that means "to fly away," like a bird that hears a loud noise. As a child, when my father, who was quite formidable, would scold me, I wanted to fly away, like a frightened bird. You may have a husband who can become formidable, especially if he is trying to shield himself from opening up his heart. Now that you are a woman, and a woman who knows that God is real, don't fly away. Hansen says:

> If the woman will stay in relationship, stay open, and not respond by
> retreating again into her own inner self-protectiveness, life and healing
> will eventually begin to come forth.[7]

Remember how, after God spoke to Lori in the shower, she shared her innermost heart with her husband? She honestly told Bob how she had failed God. Bob said, "I saw my wife broken." Her openness spoke to him and she received his help. Bob has also been able to make himself vulnerable to Lori. Together, as partners, as coheirs, they have encouraged each other to set their hope in God, and have helped each other back to the road to which God has called them. Obviously, it is easier to share with a godly man like Bob than it is to share with some men, yet there is a secret to breaking down the walls of communication with any man.

USE WORD PICTURES

In *The Language of Love*, John Trent and Gary Smalley ask:

> Can a wife find a method to penetrate her husband's natural defenses
> and get her point across so he will long remember it? . . . YES! Largely

unused in marriages, homes, friendships, and businesses is a tool that can supercharge communication and change lives. This concept is as old as ancient kings but is so timeless that is has been used throughout the ages in every society. It's a powerful communication method we call **emotional word pictures**.[8]

Recently at a Heritage Keepers conference I shared a word picture I used with my husband, Steve. It was when we were returning from Thailand after adopting our new daughter, Beth. We had toured her orphanage and seen hundreds of children who were still without homes. Though they had tugged at my heart, I definitely felt I had all I could handle. She was our fifth child, and I had a jam-packed speaking and writing schedule.

As we flew home from Bangkok with her, I exchanged smiles with her, as that was our only common language. The small child in the seat in front of us peered over the top of the seat and asked her, "What happened to your arm?" I was thankful Beth didn't understand English. I told him, "She doesn't know. She was just a baby and she can't remember." (Beth was abandoned after her arm had been amputated.) He stared with round eyes at her empty sleeve until his mother pulled him down, shushed him, and buckled him up. Sometimes, when I glanced at Beth, I saw tears glistening. It was clear she was frightened. And so was I. Continually I was pushing those anxieties down with prayer. Beth also experienced airplane sickness. (She'd only been in a car a few times—and of course, never in a plane.) Sometime during that anxious trip Steve leaned over to me and said, "Some of those little boys in Beth's orphanage were sure cute."

How in the world could I help my husband understand that this was definitely not the time to talk to me about adopting more children?

A word picture!

I asked the Lord to give me a good one and He did. This was our conversation.

Honey—look out at that airplane wing. Imagine that I am out there. I am hanging on for dear life. The wind is whipping my hair, my legs are flying out behind me, and my fingers are slipping on the cold metal. Though I want so much to keep up with you in your Christian walk, I'm afraid I'm going to plummet to my death!

Steve's eyes widened. *Is that how you are feeling?*

Yes! Then, after a deep breath, I qualified my answer: *But I have given my whole life to the Lord—and if He shows me we should adopt more children—then I will.*

Steve put his arm around me. But before he could say anything, I remembered Esther's great line as she marched boldly toward God's call on her life. I delivered it with as much drama as I could:

And if I perish, I perish.

We both laughed. Yet I helped my husband understand, through a word picture, that I needed not another challenge, but help. Instead of flying away like a frightened bird, I shared my heart with a word picture.

Steve and I, like Abraham and Sarah, are coheirs. Together we are raising a child who has been severely wounded by life. Together we are setting our hope in God and not giving way to hysterical fears. And together we are seeing God's power and grace bring healing to Beth.

The Christian life is the most exciting, fulfilling life on earth. Yet it is not easy. It is vital that we stay in step with the Spirit, neither lagging behind or running ahead.

After Heritage Keepers had their first wonderfully successful conference in Wichita with speakers like Marge Caldwell and John Trent, Bob and Lori got ahead of God. Lori said, "We were so excited we ran ahead. We didn't listen to God's full sentence."

Running ahead brought them into a full-fledged crisis.

Panning for Heritage Gold

☀ Icebreaker: What is one of your most frequent fears?

1. What stood out to you from the text and Scriptures in the sixth chapter? Why?

2. Read 1 Peter 2:13–3:7 as an overview. List any initial observations. Look for patterns, commands, and comparisons.

☀ When Peter points to Sarah as a model, he refers to the time when she called Abraham "lord." It is important, therefore, to study that passage. It's a fascinating story.

3. Read Genesis 17:15-17 and describe exactly how Abraham responded to the news that Sarah would bear him a son. (v. 17)

4. Read Genesis 18:1–19:1. Look for clues as to the identity of the "three visitors." What do you discover? Give verse references.

The visitors were two angels (see 19:1) and the Lord. (If you missed this, look again, for there are many clues!)

5. How did Sarah show her respect for Abraham in this chapter? (Give verse references.)

If you are married, how do you show respect for your husband?

6. Read Genesis 18:9-15 slowly.

    A. Since Abraham had already been told of the impending miracle, what was the purpose of this visit?

    B. How does this show God valued Sarah?

C. How did Sarah respond to the news?

D. What significance do you see in the fact that, in talking to herself, Sarah refers to Abraham as her master (or her lord)?

E. When God read Sarah's thoughts and rebuked her, why do you think the rebuke was so mild?

She laughed not out of cocky arrogance but because a life of long disappointment had taught her not to clutch at straws. Hopelessness, not pride, underlay her unbelief. Her self-restraint in not openly expressing her doubts and the sadness behind them go far to explain the gentleness of the divine rebuke.[9]

G. How did the rebuke clinch the argument? How do you think Sarah felt at this point?

I believe the whole passage shows God's great love for Sarah. He came, I believe, especially to help her faith through His Word.

7. Share a time when a rebuke of the Lord through His Spirit or through His Word helped you.

 Read 1 Peter 3:1-6.

8. Describe winning behavior.

9. Contrast the above to behavior that is not persuasive, as found in 2 Timothy 2:23-26.

Is there an application for your life?

10. How did the holy women of old make themselves beautiful? Write down *everything* you discover.

11. Chuck Swindoll says the word *obeyed* means "paid careful attention to." If you are married, give evidence that you do this with your husband.

12. How do we become a daughter of Sarah? What does this mean?

13. What are some ways to gently increase communication with a man who throws up a protective wall?

Read 1 Peter 3:14.

14. Again, Peter talks about not giving way to fear. Whom should we not fear and whom should we fear? Why? (See also the original quote in Isaiah 8:11-14.) Find all the reasons you can and give verse references.

The *Word Biblical Commentary* translates Isaiah 8:13:
You may call Yahweh of Hosts "a conspirator"!
He is your fear! He is your dread!

15. Find more reasons to fear God in 1 Peter 3:10-12. (See also the original quote in Psalm 34.)

16. Do you live your life in the fear of man or in the fear of God? Give evidence.

17. Is there a fear you could surrender to God? What is it?

18. What has God impressed on your heart through this lesson?

PRAYER TIME:

Share a fear you have in prayer and allow your sisters to support you, using the wisdom they have gleaned from 1 Peter.

Seven

We're going to lose everything. Our costs are into six digits and women are not buying tickets. We're going to lose our house. O Lord, what should we do? Should we cancel? Should we refund the money so we don't lose even more?

LORI'S THOUGHTS SHORTLY BEFORE THE DENVER HERITAGE KEEPERS CONFERENCE: APRIL, 1997

Stay in Step with the Spirit

By February of '96, all the speakers were in place. *Christianity Today* got wind of Heritage Keepers and wrote about it in the July issue. When the doors opened for the first Heritage Keepers conference five months later in Wichita, excited women flooded in, filling up the seats. Lori reminisced: "I sat in the front row and could totally see and feel God's presence."

One of the most moving moments of the day occurred when Randy Storms, who is paralyzed from the waist down, asked his wife Suzi to come out on stage. Randy had honored Suzi with his words, telling of how God had gifted him with this wonderful wife at a time when he thought no woman would ever want him. Suzi, a beautiful, slim blond, came out. Looking into her eyes, Randy said, "I would like to wash your feet." A silence came over the women as Suzi placed a basin of water in her husband's lap and removed her sandals. She submitted first her left foot to her husband who bathed it and dried it gently. Then the right. When he finished the audience leaped to its feet and applauded. Suzi gave her husband a hug and left the stage. A woman from Topeka, quoted in *The Wichita Eagle*, commented, "In relationships today, you seldom see a love like that expressed in front of three thousand people."

At the end of the day Bob Beckler gave an altar call, and women poured to the front to give their lives to Christ. Lori said, "I kept thinking, *Thank You, Thank You, Lord. Thank You so much for tugging on my heart, for pulling me back in Your path. Here I was going my own way and You got my attention.*" Lori's eyes filled at the memory and asked a question we should think about every day of our lives: "What can satisfy like the joy of being used of God?" When we are in step with the Spirit there is a joy and a peace that surpasses all the treasures in the world.

The next week the phone was ringing off the hook with requests for Heritage Keepers to come to Oklahoma City, to Denver, to Portland, and to more cities. "This," Lori said, "is where we got ahead of God. We were so excited we ran ahead of Him. We didn't listen to His full sentence."

LISTENING TO GOD'S FULL SENTENCE

As women, we often can correctly finish each other's sentences, demonstrating the beautiful fluidity of women's friendships. Linguists call this style "rapport talk" in contrast to the male style of "report talk." At a recent Heritage Keepers conference I asked women to huddle in groups of two or three to respond to a question. The arena absolutely *hummed* as women immediately connected.

When we are talking to other women it can be beautiful and satisfying to engage in "rapport talk." But when we try to finish God's sentences for Him, it can be dangerous. His ways and His thoughts are so above ours that we cannot anticipate His response in the same way we can with our girlfriends. We've got to learn to be still, to listen carefully, before we go running off into the activities of the day.

Solomon gives us the proper attitude toward God in Ecclesiastes 5:1.

Guard your steps when you go to the house of God. Go near to listen rather than to offer the sacrifice of fools, who do not know that they do wrong.

Nancy Messner, the pianist for many of Moody Bible Institute's women's conferences, laughed as she told me about her almost three-year-old granddaughter. "Because their phone has an automatic dialer, my granddaughter can push just one number and reach me. It is such a surprise when I answer the phone, expecting to hear an adult voice, and instead I hear this tiny, tiny voice saying:

Hi Grammy! I a big girl! I wuv you! Bye.

"Before I can respond, the receiver thuds down and I'm left with a dial tone." Nancy smiled, "I guess that's how God must feel when we pray—it's all one-sided—and then we are gone."

Yesterday I was typing away in my prayer journal, which I do on my computer, pouring my heart out to God. I praised Him, I thanked Him, and I flooded Him with requests. Then I closed my file and shut down my computer. The screen darkened. Suddenly I remembered Nancy's granddaughter. I had hung up on God.

Chagrined, I turned my computer back on and keyed:

Speak, Lord. Your servant is listening.

Then I did what is so hard for me to do. I was still. He began to impress on my mind the things that mattered to Him: areas where I needed to be more responsive to Him, things that mattered to Him for me to do that day, thoughts from the psalm I had studied that morning. (The primary way He speaks to us is through His Word. As we pan for gold, looking carefully, He may surprise us with a gem for the day.) I began to type *these* thoughts in my computer. Now, I was listening to Him.

Today, when I opened up my prayer file, I saw the list of things He had impressed on my heart yesterday. Had I paid attention to Him? (The real test of listening is obedience.) I had obeyed in five areas—and disobeyed in the area that so easily besets me. (*Wouldn't you like to know what that is?*) Today I'm aiming for 100 percent. I long to listen and obey. I want to let Him finish His full sentence. When He calls, *My daughter,*

My daughter—I don't want to be talking. I want to keep in step with His Spirit. I do not want to lag behind or to run ahead.

LAGGING BEHIND

You would expect the child of Abraham and Sarah to be a spiritual giant, but Isaac was not. Pastor John Bronson describes him as "a man who showed little initiative, whose father had to find him a wife when he was middle aged." Bronson also calls Isaac "a man of trivia," for his main interest in life seemed to be his dinner menu. (See the Bible study at the end of this chapter for more about Isaac.) Later it becomes apparent that Isaac failed to instruct his son Esau in important matters, for Esau is very surprised when his parents are displeased with his pagan wives. (Genesis 28:8) Hebrews 12:16 describes Esau as godless, yet Isaac liked this son the best. Though Isaac didn't reject his heritage, neither did he embrace it with awe and appreciation. He was coasting on Abraham's faith. In *Victory over Darkness*, Neil Anderson writes:

> *One of the most dangerous and harmful detriments to your spiritual growth is passivity—putting your mind in neutral and coasting.*[1]

Perhaps Isaac was a mama's boy. It wasn't until after Sarah's death that Abraham decided it was time to find a wife for his forty-year-old son.

"A Bride for Isaac" is a fascinating story demonstrating the providence of God and His keen interest in *His heritage*. God longs for His children, His heritage, to pass on the truths to the next generation. God often calls Himself the God of Abraham, Isaac, and Jacob. Isaac was a crucial link. Would God allow the chain to be broken?

Now you can see why the story of "A Bride for Isaac" is so significant. Our perspective is limited to just this generation, but God looks at the roll of generations to come. Did Abraham realize his son needed a strong partner—someone who could stand in the gap? I don't know, but I do know Abraham had learned to lean on God. When

Abraham asked his chief servant to travel to the country of Haran to find a bride from his own relatives for Isaac, the servant stuttered: "What if the woman is unwilling to come back with me to this land?" (Genesis 24:5a)

Perhaps Abraham remembered the night God led him outside his tent, and told him:

> *Look up at the heavens and count the stars—if indeed you can count them.... So shall your offspring be.* (Genesis 15:5)

Abraham believed God, and the Scripture tells us it was counted to him as righteousness. Would God provide a bride for Isaac? Abraham knew He would. So he answered his chief servant:

> *The Lord, the God of heaven, who brought me out of my father's household and my native land and who spoke to me and promised me on oath, saying, "To your offspring I will give this land"—he will send his angel before you so that you can get a wife for my son from there.* (Genesis 24:7)

Enter Rebekah.

REBEKAH

She's been called a female Abraham: strong, energetic, and bold. Gordon Wenham writes:

> *Rebekah's willingness to leave her land and kindred shows that she is, as it were, a female Abraham, who like him will be blessed. Her name, like his, contains the consonants b and r, which begin the [Hebrew] verb "bless", a key word in this chapter* (24: 1, 27, 31, 35, 48, 60).[2]

There is humor, drama, and romance in this story. You will love digging into it in the Bible study and discussing it with your sisters in Christ. I'd like to whet your appetite here.

Abraham sent his servant with ten camels. Ten! (Can you imagine ten black limousines driving through your neighborhood?) The servant arrived at the time of day when the women of the town came to the well to draw water. How would the servant know which woman was to be Isaac's bride? He asked God for a sign.

May it be that when I say to a girl, "Please let down your jar that I may have a drink," and she says, "Drink, and I'll water your camels too"—let her be the one you have chosen for your servant Isaac. (Genesis 24:14)

Before he had even finished praying, a beautiful virgin (her type of dress probably showed her virgin status) entered with a jar on her shoulder. Rebekah not only gave him a drink, but said exactly what he had prayed she would say and then *ran* to the well, pulled up the bucket, filled her jar, and *ran* with the heavy jar filling the trough, again and again, until all ten camels were satisfied. (No slouch was she.)

And though the confirmation was strong, God gave the chief servant yet another sign. Remember, Abraham wanted a bride from his own relatives. When the servant asked Rebekah who she was, he learned she was Abraham's niece. Overwhelmed, the servant bowed down and worshiped God.

Rebekah ran home with the news. The servant and the ten camels came tromping behind. Rebekah was now wearing gold bracelets and a gold nose ring. Rebekah's greedy brother Laban was intrigued. (*A servant has this kind of money to throw around?*) The family listened to the whole story, including the part about how God had blessed Abraham abundantly and had given his son Isaac *everything* he owned. The family agreed, either from pure or impure motives, that God was leading and that Rebekah should become Isaac's bride.

The servant wanted to take her immediately, but the brother and the mother wanted her to stay "ten days or so" (some commentators think that in Middle Eastern culture those ten days "or so" could have easily stretched to a year "or so"). Rebekah's father seemed passive in the whole affair, perhaps because he was old, or perhaps because, as Gordon Wenham suggests, "he was under his wife's thumb, just as Rebekah was later to 'organize' Isaac."[3] I certainly can identify with the mother wanting to keep her daughter a little longer. Leaving and cleaving is hard, even though it is God's plan, and the pain intensifies when it is abrupt, like yanking out a loose tooth with a string. For those women who want to use Rebekah's story as a justification for marrying quickly, I would caution them. Rebekah's servant was given several unmistakable signs and Rebekah's family confirmed God's leading. When Terry Jones of Point of Grace was asked "How can I know for sure if he's the one?" she answered: *What worked for me was to wait. That's how I knew that I was in love with him.*[4] That's the same counsel Naomi gave to Ruth in Ruth 3:18: *Wait, my daughter*. If God is in a relationship, He will hold it together. You don't need to run ahead of the Spirit.

When the servant wanted to take Rebekah immediately, the tension is palpable. Both sides are firm. The servant said, without his usual graciousness: "Do not detain me, now that the Lord has granted success to my journey" (Genesis 24:56).

What did they do? The schemer Laban had an idea. Let the decision be Rebekah's. (Surely *she* will delay the departure.) But she surprised them when she said decisively, "I will go." (Genesis 24:58b)

Strong and confident. Respectful to her parents, yet not clinging to them. God's leading was clear, she had the support of her family, so she will not lag behind. It can be as disastrous to lag behind the Spirit as to run ahead, for whoever is continually watching the wind and the clouds, waiting for the *perfect* moment, will never plant and will never reap. (Ecclesiastes 11:4) Rebekah is strong, she is a woman of faith, and so she moves out. How like Abraham! Gordon Wenham writes: "If Isaac should prove to be somewhat ineffectual, Rebekah, his new wife, will be equal to the call."[5]

God cares about His heritage.

STAYING IN STEP WITH THE SPIRIT

When Isaac brought Rebekah into his late mother's tent, she was established, commentators say, as "the new Sarah." She was the next link in the chain, and she needed to be strong, especially because Isaac, unlike Abraham, was weak. Would she stay in step with the Spirit?

As with Sarah, God seems slow in fulfilling His promise for children. For twenty years Rebekah was barren. Yet, to her credit, she did not run ahead of God and take matters into her own hands by asking Isaac to sleep with one of her many maids. Instead, Isaac finally showed a little initiative and prayed on behalf of his barren wife. God answered the prayer and Rebekah conceived twins: Jacob and Esau. Even in the womb they were rivals. Rebekah's pregnancy made her so miserable she wondered if life was worth living. But again, we see spiritual strength, for her Spirit-led response to misery is to inquire of the Lord, asking Him what is happening to her. The Lord said to her:

> *Two nations are in your womb, and two peoples from within you will be separated; one people will be stronger than the other, and the older will serve the younger.* (Genesis 25:23)

Without an ultrasound Rebekah knew she was carrying twins, and that the younger would be in charge. (This story reminds me of when my friend Juanita sought the Lord for the name of the child she was expecting and had the clear impression: *Joshua*. Later, after an ultrasound, the doctor asked her if she wanted to know the sex of her eighth child. She surprised him by saying, "Well, you can tell me, but I already know it's a boy because God told me to name him Joshua." And, sure enough, Juanita gave birth to a son who is a true leader, a *Joshua*.)

If Rebekah had clung to the word God gave her in her pregnancy, I believe she could have avoided much of the heartbreak she experienced later in life. But it can be difficult, especially if you have the gifts of a leader, and especially if God seems slow in fulfilling His promise, to wait. Rebekah had done well in her youth and even in the years of her barrenness. But in Rebekah's later years, she ran ahead of God, grabbing the reins from God.

SATAN GAINS A FOOTHOLD

A pattern I have seen with the Enemy is that he longs to divide. He is a wolf who scatters the sheep, dividing believers in families and the family of God. With Rebekah and Isaac, a rift begins as the twins grow up, for each parent has a favorite twin.

> *The boys grew up, and Esau became a skillful hunter, a man of the open country, while Jacob was a quiet man, staying among the tents. Isaac, who had a taste for wild game, loved Esau, but Rebekah loved Jacob.* (Genesis 25:27-28)

It is intriguing to read between the lines in these chapters and observe the widening rift through the way all four participants refer to each other. Isaac addresses Esau tenderly, saying, *my son.* Rebekah does the same with Jacob. When Jacob talks about Esau to Rebekah, he does not say, *your son* but, *my brother.* Rebekah does the same. Somewhere along the line, Rebekah rejected Esau. Esau is left without love from his mother and without guidance from his passive father.

Parents have an enormous responsibility before God to love and to cherish each of their children and to pass on the heritage to each of their children. Each child the Lord gives us is a trust, a heritage from Him. (Psalm 127:3) If we have a favorite child and are neglecting the others, God will hold us accountable, for we have neglected His heritage.

Traditionally in the Old Testament, when the father was on his deathbed he would call for the children and bless them each with a prophetic prayer. But Isaac didn't call for *both* sons. He called his favorite son and whispered:

> *I am now an old man and don't know the day of my death. Now then, get your weapons—your quiver and bow—and go out to the open country to hunt some wild game for me. Prepare me the kind of tasty food I like and bring it to me to eat, so that I may give you my blessing before I die.* (Genesis 27:2-4)

Running Ahead of the Spirit

Rebekah, eavesdropping, was alarmed. Taking her favorite son aside, she counsels Jacob to deceive his aged and blind father by pretending to be Esau. Jacob kills a goat, binding the goatskin on his arms in order to smell and feel like his hairy brother, and goes in to his father with a tasty stew. Rebekah, in running ahead of the Spirit, made a total mess of everything, not only for her family, but for generations to come.

A wounded Esau turned on his twin. Protectively, Rebekah sends Jacob fleeing for his life. She never saw Jacob again. She and Isaac also passed on a heritage of deceit and favoritism. Jacob would have a favorite wife (Rachel) and a favorite son (Rachel's firstborn, Joseph). That favoritism would lead to one of the ugliest episodes of sibling rivalry in history. Our sin patterns have a tendency to ripple out for generations to come.

Your Choices Make a Difference

A sister conference that God has blessed greatly is Hearts at Home. This conference, begun by Jill Savage, helps young moms realize just how important their role can be for future generations. I had Sunday dinner in the home of Jill and Mark Savage recently and was enchanted by their three joyful, well-behaved children. When their two year old asked, "Please may I have my nap now?" I rolled my eyes, teasing them that this couldn't be the real world. Jill is living what she is preaching. When I spoke at Hearts at Home, I surveyed the sea of fresh faces and bright eyes. Nearly a third were pregnant. I laughed when singer Cheri Keaggy started singing a *Veggie Tale* song and suddenly thousands of voices joined her. Speaker Elise Arndt gave a wonderful illustration demonstrating how obedience or disobedience ripples through future generations. Elise told of two families from the 1700s and two contrasting *heritages*.

In the Jukes family, an atheist married an ungodly woman. From their union to the fourth generation of 1,200 known descendants came:

400 physical wrecks
310 paupers

150 criminals
7 murderers

In contrast, Jonathan Edwards was a great American preacher who married a godly woman. From their union to the fourth generation of 1,394 known descendants came:

14 college presidents
100 ministers of the Gospel, missionaries, or theologians
100 judges or lawyers
16 physicians
60 authors and editors

Offspring of the Edwards' union influenced nearly every North American industry and their spiritual influence is still being felt today.[6]

What a responsibility we have to walk in the Spirit! No wonder God is calling to each of us: *My daughter, My daughter: walk in the Spirit and you will impact generations to come.*

OKLAHOMA CITY: NOVEMBER 1996

After the first successful Heritage Keepers conference in Wichita, Lori and Bob received many invitations to come to various cities. "Sure! We'll come!" Lori said, "We planned the next in Oklahoma City in just two months and four more in '97."

"Do you think you jumped ahead of God?" I asked.

Lori nodded sadly. "We did. God has His perfect plan and His permissive plan. He can bless His permissive plan, but it is always sad to miss His best. Because we failed to wait upon Him and really listen, we jumped ahead at this point and missed His best. Speakers were booked that should not have been booked. Promises were made that were going to broken."

The conference in Oklahoma City was a tremendous success spiritually. Nearly half of the women attending went forward for salvation or recommitment.

However, following the promising beginning in Wichita, the attendance of only seven hundred women in Oklahoma City was disappointing. The Becklers had to dip into their personal savings to cover the costs. Unlike the many women's conferences that have the blessing of being backed by a successful Christian radio program or publisher, Bob and Lori did not have that kind of backing. Of course *any* ministry needs to be dependent on the Lord, but when there's no cushion, every bump is frightening. It's easy to walk by faith when the road is smooth; it's harder when the road gets bumpy and your cushion is thin.

After the conference in Oklahoma City, Bob and Lori went to Chili's for barbecued ribs with Wellington Boone, who seems to be anointed to give a good word at the right time. Though thrilled by the spiritual response that day in Oklahoma City, Bob and Lori were concerned about the numbers and the financial outlay of the conferences that lay ahead. They had contacted some well-known singers for future conferences, but the cost seemed prohibitive. Though they had never done a women's conference, Point of Grace, who had won the Dove Award as the group of the year, had expressed interest in helping them. However, Point of Grace was already booked for concerts, and the probability of being free for the upcoming Heritage Keepers conferences was slim. Lori shared all this with Wellington and sighed, tears filling her eyes.

"I can still picture Wellington," Lori smiled. "He took a rib from his plate and pointed it at me. Shaking it up and down for emphasis, he said:

Lori, there are people called to this ministry. There are people ordained to be a part of Heritage Keepers. You don't know who they are or where they live but God will bring them together in His own time.

Lori clung to that statement.

But the real valleys lay ahead.

DENVER: APRIL 1997

As they headed toward their third conference in Denver in April of

'97, the Becklers and Bowlings worked very hard, not wanting to repeat the low attendance of Oklahoma City. "We made eleven trips to Denver," Lori said, "working harder than we'd ever worked before. We went door to door and radio station to radio station." However, while there is nothing wrong with working hard or with advertising, you cannot make up in the flesh what you are lacking in the Spirit. If God is not leading, you are paddling upstream.

Despite all the work, two weeks before the Denver conference only two hundred women had signed up. Lori said, "It was tax day, April fifteenth, and Bob and I looked at each other and said: 'My goodness— what are we doing?' We were both as low as could be. Panic was growing as I thought: *We're going to lose everything. Our costs are into six digits. We're going to lose our house. O Lord, what should we do? Should we cancel? Should we refund the money so we don't lose even more?"*

Like Sarah, like Rebekah, Lori is striking, strong, resourceful, and decisive. Her faith is strong. Her mother proudly told me: "When Lori was just ten years old she kept her Bible by her bedside and read it every night. She was an unusual little girl." Lori, like the holy women of old, moves ahead where many would be fearful to go. These are all wonderful traits as long as you are walking in the Spirit. But it is also easy for people like this to begin in the Spirit and then to run ahead of God.

THE SECRET OF WALKING IN THE SPIRIT

Is there a secret to walking in the Spirit and not lagging behind or running ahead? Yes. In *Victory over the Darkness,* Neil Anderson gives the key. What matters is not a set of rules, but keeping our relationship with Christ vital. Anderson says:

Walking according to the Spirit is more a relationship than a regimen. Think about your marriage as an illustration. You may have started out relying on some rules for effective communication, meeting each other's sexual needs, etc. But if after several years you can't even talk to each other or make love without following an outline or list of steps, your marriage is still in infancy. The goal of marriage is to develop a relationship which supersedes rules.[7]

This analogy works so well—and it is the same one Scripture uses. Again and again, we are told that marriage is a mysterious reflection of the relationship between Christ and believers, whom Scripture calls "the bride of Christ." Whether it is love for a spouse or love for the Lord, what matters is that you love so deeply that you don't allow anything or anyone to block that love. When an attractive man smiles at me, I don't have to think: *The seventh commandment says, "You shall not commit adultery."* Instead, I know I would never do anything to hurt Steve that way. I love my husband intensely, and so I obey the rule without even thinking about it. That's how God longs for us to love Him. Instead of saying, *Oh, I've got to read my three chapters in the Bible this morning,* we wake up longing to be with Him. Instead of thinking, *I have to turn off this intriguing but questionable TV show because God wouldn't like it,* we should think, *If I allow this into my heart, it will block the wonderful flow of the Spirit, and nothing, absolutely nothing, is worth that!*

Neil Anderson says there is a simple test to know if you are walking in the Spirit. Those who walk in the Spirit have the fruit of the Spirit. (See Galatians 5:22-23.) If you don't have peace, joy, and love—then you are out of step.[8] If the fruit is missing in your life, ask God to search your heart and show you what is blocking His Spirit from flowing. Then confess, receive Christ's forgiveness, and get back on the right path.

When we get back on the path, the Lord will also help us with the messes that departing from the path created. God will not abandon us. Often, mercifully, God will lend a hand in the form of a friend.

IF ONE FALLS DOWN, HER FRIEND CAN HELP HER UP

Betty and Lowell Bowling stopped by two weeks before the Denver conference to find Lori and Bob at an emotional bottom. "Mom and Dad," Lori said weeping, "I think we're going to cancel the conference in Denver."

Betty said, "Cancel? Two weeks before? Women are counting on you."

Tears streamed down Lori's face. She was overwhelmed. Before Betty and Lowell left that night they embraced their children, promising to pray. They prayed off and on throughout the night. Likewise, other members of the family prayed. Lori's sister Kim and Kim's husband, Bryce, cried out to God, pleading for wisdom, for *His plan*. The next morning Betty and Lowell had a plan and a peace that it was from God. Confidently, they drove to the bank to take out their life's savings, the savings they had planned to use for retirement the following year.

I asked Betty, "What were you feeling?"

She smiled. "I remember thinking—*well, we brought nothing with us into the world and we're not going to take anything out—so we might as well use this for God's Kingdom.*"

Lori said, "When Mom and Dad came over ready to invest in Denver we were firm. I said, 'No way. We are not going to do that. We would rather lose our house than take your retirement savings.'"

But her dad said, "We love you, Lori and Bob, but we aren't doing this for you. We're doing this for the Lord. God has been working in our hearts. We believe in this ministry. If you don't take the money then you are not letting us obey God."

Personally, I respect the Bowlings immensely for doing what they believed to be right and not giving way to fear. They felt promises had been made to the women who had bought tickets, to the people working behind the scenes in Denver, and to the speakers and musicians. Since they were a part of the Heritage Keepers team, they felt a responsibility to help the ministry keep their word. When David asks:

Lord, who may dwell in your sanctuary?
Who may live on your holy hill?

God answers with a list of characteristics which flow from those who are walking in the Spirit, including:

He whose walk is blameless
and who does what is righteous ...
who keeps his oath
even when it hurts. (Psalm 15:2, 4)

How much was keeping their word going to hurt the Bowlings? Lori said, "It's one thing to hurt for yourself—it's quite another to see that your choices may mean tremendous sacrifice to those you love. My hope was that the numbers would turn around as the Denver conference drew very near. But about a week before, when the numbers *still* weren't coming in, I was at my lowest low. I went over to Central Community one morning and into the chapel. I was in there a long time sobbing before the Lord. I said, *Lord, what am I doing to the people who have loved me all my life? And they love You, Lord. What is happening?* Then I went into Bob's office and sobbed. Pretty soon one of the pastors from Central Community came in. We are down on our knees, broken, confessing. For forty-five minutes we prayed. Then I left. Though shaky, I felt better. I reminded myself that after Denver Heritage Keepers would have a return engagement to Wichita, and that was likely to go well. But then I thought about the conference following on its heels: Indianapolis. Unknown territory. *O Lord* (I was praying constantly now), *sustain us. Give us some encouragement. We just want to do what You want us to do.* Lori walked to her car, and sat in it for a moment, stilling her heart. Then she dialed her voice-mail from her car phone.

When she listened, she could hardly believe her ears.

Panning for Heritage Gold

☀ Icebreaker: Are you more likely to be late, early, or on time? What does this tell you about yourself?

1. What stood out to you from the text and Scriptures in the seventh chapter? Why?

2. False teachers came to the early Christians and told them they needed to be circumcised. Today we often try to walk according to rules instead of according to the Spirit. *Read the short book of Galatians.* Afterward, write down what you think it means to walk in the Spirit. Give verse references.

☼ 3. Rather than a formula, walking in the Spirit has to do with a relationship. When you love the Lord you listen to Him, trust Him, and obey Him. As a review, how did the following people model this or fail to model this in these passages?

A. Genesis 3:2-6

B. Genesis 4:6-8

C. Genesis 15:1-6 and Romans 4:18-22

D. 1 Peter 3:5-6

4. In Galatians 2:20, Paul summarizes the secret of staying in step with the Spirit. What is it?

Read Galatians 4:21-31.

5. Summarize Paul's analogy. What does it mean?

What is our heritage, our inheritance? (Galatians 4:3–5:1)

6. How would you describe your love relationship with the Lord right now? Is self blocking His Spirit?

7. Read Genesis 24. Find all the evidences you can for Abraham, Abraham's chief servant, and Rebekah staying in step with the Spirit. Give verse references.

8. What do you learn about Isaac from the following passages?

    A. Genesis 25:18-21

    B. Genesis 25:28

    C. Genesis 26:1-9

D. Genesis 27:1-4

E. Genesis 28:6-9

9. Why do you think God chose Rebekah for Isaac?

10. Whether a woman is single, married to a passive man like Isaac, or a giant like Abraham, God calls her to stand in the gap. Find everything possible about passing on our heritage to the next generation from Deuteronomy 6.

☼ 11. Read Genesis 27. Describe how Rebekah walked in the flesh instead of in the Spirit. What were the consequences to her, to Jacob, and to Esau? Give verse references.

12. What do you learn about Esau from Hebrews 12:16-17? Is there a warning for you?

Esau seemed to love food more than God. Why, do you think?

13. What have been some of the consequences in your life when you have walked in the flesh instead of the Spirit?

When you have lagged behind God?

When you have run ahead?

14. One of the most reliable ways to know if we are walking in the Spirit is by our love relationship with God and with others. Meditate on Galatians 5:13-15. What do you learn?

15. Meditate on Galatians 5:16-18. What should be our focus and why?

16. How does Paul summarize walking according to the Spirit in Galatians 5:24-25?

17. What has God shown you through this lesson?

PRAYER TIME:

An effective way to pray is to pray through Scripture, making it personal. It is vital that we pray for our character, as well as our circumstances. Pair off and open your Bible to Galatians 5:22-26. For example, Amy might pray:

> *Please help me so abide in You that love and joy flows from me. May those close to me at work see You in me. Help me to crucify my sinful nature, especially my struggle with envy, and to stay in step with Your Spirit.*

Then Meg might say: *I agree*, and continue by praying through the passage for herself, making it personal.

---

Eight

*You are my hiding place; you will protect me from trouble
and surround me with songs of deliverance.*

PSALM 32:7

Point of Grace: Passing on a Godly Heritage

*L*ori dialed into the voice-mail on her car phone and heard David Breen, who is married to Shelley of Point of Grace. Lori held her breath, listening carefully:

Hi Lori. This is David. I have the confirmation for August eighth in Wichita for Heritage Keepers. And—about Indianapolis for September twentieth. We can come, after all. You see, Denise is pregnant—the baby is due in October, and the place we were going to be is too far away from home— it's too risky—but Indy would work great. Do you still want us for Indy?

Lori leaned back and closed her eyes. *O Lord, I am unworthy of this kindness. Thank You. Thank You.*

One of the themes we see rolling through Abraham, Isaac, and Jacob, and right up into our generation is that despite the fallibility of God's chosen people, God is a God of grace. He keeps reaching out to us because we are His heritage. Though He disciplines us, He will never forsake us.

Bob and Lori and the staff of Heritage Keepers had made mistakes. They had run ahead of God. There were times when they had been lacking in the humility, prayer, and faith that is so pleasing to God. But God did not abandon them, and when they confessed their sin in true repentance, falling on their faces before Him, He opened the floodgates to bless them.

Failing God is wrong. But not admitting it is worse. When Denise Jones of Point of Grace remembers being disciplined as a child she says: "We were taught early on that the only thing worse than being up to no good was denying it afterward."[1] Isn't that a powerful spiritual principle to impress on your children's hearts? Learning that, not only as children, but as children of God, is one of the most vital lessons of life. Instead of persisting in the darkness, going deeper and deeper, we must learn to humble ourselves and admit our wrong. When this is the practice of our lives, we experience joy and peace. When David kept silent about his sin, his "bones wasted away," God's hand was "heavy upon him," and his "strength was sapped." But when he acknowledged his sin openly, God became his "hiding place," surrounding him with "songs of deliverance." (Psalm 32:2-7)

WHY POINT OF GRACE?

When Bob and Lori acknowledged their sin, falling on their faces before God, God became their hiding place and surrounded them with songs of deliverance—specifically, through Point of Grace!

Why did God bring this group, in particular, on board? I can only speculate, but certainly the popularity of Point of Grace was a wonderful boost to attendance at Heritage Keepers. It is at least interesting that their participation became possible moments after Bob and Lori and the Heritage Keepers team were broken, praying on their faces before the Lord. I also think that experiencing this grace from God in their time of need may have softened Bob and Lori toward giving grace to Sandi Patty in her time of need in the following year.

But perhaps the main reason God called Point of Grace to Heritage Keepers was because each of these four women grew up in a godly home, enriched by a godly heritage. The first few times they came to Heritage Keepers, they would often share about their upbringing, and the values that had been instilled in their hearts. They would often ask for prayer from the audience, for they had been taught the power of prayer as little girls. Shelley Breen, who is often the spokeswoman for the group, asked for prayer concerning the songs they would choose for their new album. Heather Floyd, who was the only one still unmarried, asked for prayer that she would remain pure as "an older single."

At a return engagement to Heritage Keepers in Wichita in April of 1999, Shelley did the introductions, as usual. When she introduced Heather, she said, "Heather got engaged last week!" The audience cheered loudly. Shelley continued: "Her fiancé woke her up in the morning, knelt down beside her bed on the bus, and asked her if she'd like to change her last name!" Heather proudly stretched out her hand under the lights. Only the expressions of Shelley, Denise, and Terry outglittered the rock on Heather's third finger.

There was more excitement to come, for it was at that particular conference that all four of their mothers were in attendance. With anticipation, Denise called them out on stage:

We do a lot of women's conferences but this one is very special to us because we all grew up in Christian homes with our main role models being our moms, who have just loved us, have been there for us, and have encouraged us along the way. They're our biggest cheerleaders. It is really special because Heritage Keepers wanted to bring our moms here today, and they have never, all four, been at a concert of ours together, and they're here! Here come our moms—our heroes!

Then Shelley, Denise, Heather, and Terry shared a little about their heritage, while their moms smiled through their tears. It was a tender time, as each daughter broke down, and pretty soon the whole auditorium was in tears. Definitely a woman thing!

Shelley boldly seized the mike, as the first to introduce her mom: "I take after my dad because my mom is nice and sweet." (We laughed.) "I can honestly tell you there was never a day when I didn't see the love of Christ in my mom and dad." (*Wow,* I thought. *What a tribute!*) Shelley smiled at her mom and said, "When I was a little girl I would promise, every Sunday, to be good in 'big church.' But then I'd get bored and stand up on the wooden pew and start tapping my black patent leather shoes until someone would take me to the nursery." (We laughed again. It wasn't hard to picture pint-sized Shelley as a mischievous little girl.) Then Shelley became serious, and said: "I know some of you moms are thinking, *Today is really hard for me because my son or daughter doesn't want to go to church. I feel like I have to make them.* But that's okay. **Make them.** Because some of that stuff is going to stick!"

It was apparent, as Shelley continued sharing, that her parents' desire for her was not so much that she be dedicated to church, or to a particular denomination, but that she fall in love with Jesus. Her family was Lutheran, but when Shelley wanted to go with a friend to the Baptist church on Sunday nights and sing in their big youth choir, they supported her. ("That's where I learned all my Sandi Patty songs," Shelley enthused.) "Every Sunday morning we'd go to Hope Lutheran, and nearly every Sunday night they'd come hear me sing at the Baptist church. It didn't matter what church, what denomination, as long as I was going—they were really, really supportive. I know a lot of my friends' parents wouldn't have been that way."

It touched me to see how each young woman honored her mother, in a day when respect, honor, and gratitude for parents is becoming increasingly rare. Heather took the mike next, and said, "It is such an honor to be standing with my mom on stage. I've learned so much from my mother. One of the greatest things Mom taught me was how to dig into the Word of God." Heather hesitated, obviously wrestling with emotion. "I remember when I was young and trying to be cool and thinking, *I don't want to be like my mom.*" Heather wiped her eyes and looked directly at her mother. "Today, I want to be just like my mom."

The tears were falling freely on and off stage. Kleenex was being passed. Heather then told the audience that she was very emotional, not just because her mom was there, and not just because she had gotten engaged last week, but because she was getting married in six days! Then she said, quickly and vulnerably: "I'm not pregnant! Just so you know! I am still a virgin and I'm waiting for that!" The thousands of women burst into huge applause. I thought, as I'm sure many others did: *God gave Heather the strength she requested. And how different from the standards today.* The purity and the honor that we were seeing lived out before us was a tribute to the power of a godly home.

The group teased Heather's mom, Brenda, calling her "Preacher Mom," but it was a teasing that showed great respect. Brenda then preached a little, saying, "It is such a joy being a mom. It is such a joy sharing Jesus' love so the next generation will know. It's the greatest gift you can give your children, because He is the Way, the Truth, and the Life."

Terry is the member who, in her childhood, faced deep valleys, as her dad spent time in prison. Through tears Terry said: "I'm just absolutely the luckiest girl in the world to have this mom as my mommy. We've been through a lot and she's shown me strength of character in many ways. I want to be just like you, Mom."

Then Terry's mom, Bonnie, took the mike and honored the daughters. "We've seen these girls grow and develop in the admonition of the Lord, and we're so grateful." Then she continued, reminiscing of when her daughters were young. Every morning they would pray together for missionaries, for each other, and for their day. At night they would read from a devotional. "One of the devotionals we often used was *Little Visits With God.*" Bonnie laughed and exchanged knowing smiles with Terry. "At the end there were discussion questions, and inevitably, Terry would get the question, 'What is it that you need to confess before God that has happened today?' I think one of the reasons these gals have stayed together so long is because they've learned to keep short accounts and confess to one another."

Denise said, "There are friends in your life who mean the world to you, but my mom has been my best friend growing up."

Shelley quickly interrupted, "I thought *I* was your best friend!"

Denise chuckled, but continued, undaunted: "My mom always did stuff with me, encouraged me, and taught me to love music. Sometimes she drove me crazy, like when I'd be mad and she would get out her Bible and pray with me. I'd want to say, 'I DON'T FEEL LIKE PRAYING!' But I want to say that I have seen my mom live what she teaches."

Then Denise began to cry, describing some of the losses her mom, Janice, had faced in the last year, and of how she had struggled with depression. "We lost both my grandpas within four days of each other. … It's been a difficult year, but what has been encouraging to me is that Mom hasn't given up hope. I see her continue to love God and let God work in her life. And that is amazing to me—that God continues to work in all of our lives. She's been so special and it's been a privilege now, for me to be able to encourage my mom, since she's encouraged me my whole life."

Each tribute impressed on our hearts the enormous value of being a godly mother or mentor, and of how our lives can ripple out to the generations to come.

Although we can teach the next generation, there are no "second or third generation Christians." Each generation has to make a choice, for faith doesn't flow through the blood. Denise, Terry, Shelley, and Heather each had to individually place their trust in Christ and grow in Him. Likewise, Spencer and Cole, the baby boys they are now bouncing on their knees behind stage, will one day make a choice to embrace or reject their heritage.

Jacob had a grandfather who was a mighty man of faith, and his parents, though they made mistakes, also had faith. Yet Jacob was a prodigal who seemed to have picked up the negative characteristics of the preceding generation, but not the positive. He chose, as a young man, to go his own way.

Yet God called Himself the God of Abraham, Isaac, and Jacob. Jacob was His heritage—and God was not going to let go. He went to extraordinary measures to get Jacob's attention.

JACOB'S LADDER

"Jacob's Ladder" is an American campfire tradition. I sang it as a Girl Scout, but was clueless concerning the meaning. *What is Jacob's ladder?* I thought fleetingly. But I didn't twist my ten-year-old brain, I simply sang with the other Girl Scouts as we roasted marshmallows under a canopy of constellations.

"Jacob's ladder" was an amazing vision God gave to Jacob one night when he was out "camping," on the run from the brother he had wronged. With a stone for a pillow, Jacob slept under the stars. And then:

He saw a stairway resting on the earth, with its top reaching to heaven, and the angels of God were ascending and descending on it. There above it stood the Lord, and he said: "I am the Lord, the God of your father Abraham and the God of Isaac. I will give you and your descendants the land on which you are lying. Your descendants will be like the dust of the earth, and you will spread out to the west and to the east, to the north and to the south. All peoples on earth will be blessed through you and your offspring. I am with you and will watch over you wherever you go, and I will bring you back to this land. I will not leave you until I have done what I have promised you." (Genesis 28:12-15)

Did Jacob deserve this amazing glimpse of God and His angels? Did he deserve the promise that he would be blessed with descendants, with land, with a return to his home, and with the presence of the Lord? He surely did not. He was a cheat and a liar. His very name, Jacob, means supplanter—always trying to get things for himself. But God was the God of Abraham, Isaac, and Jacob. Those of us who are mothers can identify. Our children may absolutely break our hearts, but we are not likely to forsake them. We keep reaching out to them because they are our babies.

Jacob's reaction to the vision shows how deep-seated his sin was. Though he is temporarily awestruck, he quickly bounces back, in true Jacob form. It is as though he takes a deep breath and thinks, *Wow! This is great! Not only am I clever, good-looking, and rich—now I've got God as my ally!* Bargaining was in his blood, as you will see in his response to God:

> *If God will be with me and will watch over me on this journey I am taking and will give me food to eat and clothes to wear so that I return safely to my father's house, then the Lord will be my God and this stone that I have set up as a pillar will be God's house, and of all that you give me I will give you a tenth.* (Genesis 28:20-22)

Fritz Ridenour paraphrased Jacob's response:

> *God, if you stick by me and give me what I want, then you shall indeed be my God. Why, I'll even* tithe![2]

Though it seems laughable to try to use the One who made the universe for our purposes, people do it all the time. Carol, a poised brunette attending the Indianapolis Heritage Keepers, tells of bargaining with God before she put her trust in Christ. "I had a neighbor who kept telling me Jesus was the answer. When I thought I might be having a miscarriage, I cried: 'Jesus, save my baby! If you do, I'll give fifty dollars to C.A.R.E.!' God saved my baby, but I reneged on my vow. It took twenty more years, and the death of my young husband, before I would take Jesus seriously."

Jacob said "**If** You stick by me, then you can be my God." In *Night Wrestling*, Leslie Williams writes:

> *Like the rest of us, Jacob had a lot to learn about a covenant with God—that we cannot control the terms of the contract or the circumstances of our lives, and that once we claim the Lord as our God, we belong to Him and not vice-versa.*[3]

How merciful of God not to strike us down in our arrogance. Even a vision of angels ascending and descending on a stairway to heaven only made a temporary dent in Jacob's ego. He still had no idea of the awesomeness of God.

WHO AM I?

I love it when Point of Grace gently sings the medley "Who Am I?"

We are like grasshoppers compared to an awesome God, yet He has bent down and offered us grace. "Who Am I?" contains the lyrics to John Newton's classic:

Amazing grace! How sweet the sound—
That saved a wretch like me

I believe one of the reasons these beautiful, talented, and now successful young women have been able (at least as of this point) to keep their feet on the ground is because their parents impressed on their hearts, from the time they were little, something of the awesomeness of God. We may dazzle each other with our beauty, talent, cleverness, or success, but we certainly don't dazzle God. After all, He was the One who bestowed those gifts upon us. It pleases Him when we realize He is the Giver and we are the receivers and respond with our adoration and faithfulness. Who am I? I am His daughter, a child loved by God—everything I have is because of Him. I can only bow before Him, love Him, and serve Him.

Though we can't dazzle God with our talent, we can please Him with our love. During the altar call at Heritage Keepers, I glimpsed Heather, in the dark shadows behind the curtain, bowed in fervent prayer. I thought about how many altar calls she has seen, yet her passion was undiminished. Heather has an amazing voice with an incredible range. But that isn't what pleases Jesus, for He gave Heather her voice. What pleases Him in Heather, in any of us, is her love for Him. Who is Heather? Who are any of us? We are His daughters, His heritage. We can't give Him anything He hasn't first given us. All we can do is bow before Him and adore Him.

If we don't love God passionately, He will woo us, as He wooed Jacob. If, after wooing us, we try to use Him instead of love Him, as Jacob did, then He may wound us, because He wants a refined love.

GOD WANTS OUR PURE LOVE

Jacob needed a lot of refining. Many of his impurities had been passed down from the preceding generation, for his mother Rebekah (and his Uncle Laban) had used tricks and manipulations to get what they wanted. God decided it was time to cleanse the conduit. He wanted to change *Jacob*, the man who thought he was in control of his life, to *Israel*, which means *God rules*. What would be God's method? He was going to allow Jacob to be hurt the way he had hurt—and He was going to use an absolutely breathtaking woman.

THE KIND OF WOMAN WHO MAKES MEN WEEP

When I look at Terry, Denise, Heather, and Shelley with their gorgeous faces, stunning figures, creamy skin, and luxurious hair, I think, *Lord, is that really fair?* Perhaps that's how the women of Haran felt when they saw Rachel. She was so beautiful she made men weep. (I've always wanted to be the kind of woman who would make men weep!) When Jacob saw Rachel he kissed her and began to weep aloud!

One woman disagreed with my interpretation of Jacob's tears, saying: "Dee—don't you think he was weeping because he was so glad to have arrived safely at his uncle's home?"

"In part," I said, "but I also think it is pretty evident Rachel's face and figure turned Jacob to putty." It isn't long before Jacob is bargaining with Rachel's father for his daughter's hand:

> *I'll work for you seven years in return for your younger daughter Rachel.* (Genesis 29:18)

Laban, however, was twice the cheat Jacob ever was. Quickly, Laban agreed to give Jacob a daughter for seven years of work, without naming *which* daughter. All along, I suspect, Laban planned to pawn off his homely older daughter, Leah, and then get an extra seven years of labor from Jacob for Rachel's hand.

Leah's name means *cow* and Rachel's name means *ewe*. (Appropriate, commentators say, for the daughters of a herdsman!) Leah's eyes were lacking in sparkle, like blank cow eyes, and her physical beauty paled in comparison to her younger sister who was "lovely in form, and beautiful." (Genesis 29:17) Jacob worked diligently for seven years and then went to Laban, and, rather undiplomatically, said:

> *Give me my wife. My time is completed, and I want to lie with her.* (Genesis 29:21)

At this point we have to fill in the gaps with our imagination, for we are not told exactly how Laban managed to pull off the dirty trick he had planned. Obviously, he needed Leah's cooperation. I imagine Laban went to her and said something like:

> *Honey, tonight Jacob thinks he is going to marry Rachel. But he's not. We need to get you married. We are going to veil you heavily. Don't say anything during the ceremony, and don't lift your veil until you get into his dark tent! During the night, don't let on that you are Leah. We need to get this marriage consummated. Now, in the morning, he may be a bit upset—but just leave him to me. I'm going to give him Rachel too—but only after he has married you.*

I think Leah should have said, "Dad, I love you—but I can't do that before God. Rachel is my sister! Let's just let her have what God has given her, which is Jacob's love. I think God has a plan for me too." But, instead, she must have said, "Good idea, Dad!"

I imagine all during their wedding night Jacob whispered *Rachel, Oh, Rachel.* How humiliated he must have felt when the morning light dawned on homely Leah's face.

To the Wicked, God Shows Himself Shrewd

Do you see what God allowed? Jacob is the one who dressed up like his brother to get what belonged to his brother. Jacob is the one who went along with his mother's evil plan. Now Leah has dressed up like her sister to get what belonged to her sister. Leah went along with her father's evil plan. Jacob now knows what it feels like to be disgraced, deceived, and deprived. The just retribution of God is a pattern in the Jacob story that you will discover in the Bible study. It gives me a healthy fear of God. If I am unmerciful toward someone who has failed, might not God teach me compassion by allowing me to fail in the same way? Or if I hurt someone with gossip or deceit, might not He choose to teach me, His *heritage*, a life lesson? He allows us to reap what we sow because He cares about our character. So when I am suffering, I need to ask myself if this could be a loving response from God, for Hebrews 12:5-6 warns:

> *My son, do not make light of the Lord's discipline, and do not lose heart when he rebukes you, because the Lord disciplines those he loves, and he punishes everyone he accepts as a son.*

How do I know if I have walked into the darkness and if God is disciplining me? Circumstances may not be a reliable guide, for you can be right with God and still have adverse circumstances, as has been true of many martyrs, and of Jesus Himself. A more reliable guide is the presence or absence of the fruit of the Spirit. Paul wrote, even when he faced prison and floggings:

> *We know sorrow, yet our joy is inextinguishable.* (2 Corinthians 6:10 J.B. PHILLIPS)

When the peace and joy is gone in my life, I know it is time to examine my life. Charles Spurgeon says: "Holiness is happiness."[4]

BEING RESPONSIVE TO GOD'S DISCIPLINE

Sandi Patty has been through tremendous storms in her life, storms, which, she says frankly, were nobody's fault but her own. But Sandi responded to the discipline of the Lord, humbling herself, confessing her sin, and accepting the discipline suggested by her church. (That story is coming in chapter 10.) I see God restoring Sandi because of her repentant heart, and I see the joy and peace returning to Sandi's life, and a sweetness which is so endearing. One scene, in particular, comes to mind.

Point of Grace was on stage at Heritage Keepers. Sandi Patty and Kathy Troccoli sat in the first row in the audience, and I was directly behind them. Before Point of Grace did an absolutely side-splitting musical rendition of Noah, Shelley looked out at Sandi, who had been her "idol," she said, during her growing up years. Shelley said, "I can hardly believe this is happening. I sang Sandi Patty songs growing up. We've had Sandi Patty and Kathy Troccoli on pedestals, and now they're watching us!"

After the skit, I saw Sandi lean over and whisper something to Kathy. Then Sandi and Kathy jumped up, ran to the stage, and bowed down low, over and over, to express light-hearted but sincere admiration to Point of Grace. Shelley, particularly, came unglued! Later I asked Sandi what had motivated her. She said, "They were wonderful—that skit deserved some kind of accolade. And you're only the new kid on the block just so long." The desire on Sandi's part to encourage these younger women showed to me a maturity and a sweetness that come only from God.

It's easy, if your eyes are not on God, to feel threatened or envious of the talent of the next generation. They say we tend to envy those whose gifts are closest to our own. But if your eyes are on God, you see things differently, for you are looking for His praise instead of the praise of man.

Our lives are short, we are just a link in the chain. We are, as Sandi said, "the new kid on the block just so long." If we can mentor and encourage the next generation, we extend our influence and please God.

Our lives are so fleeting. We are, Scripture says, like a vapor. Only one psalm is attributed to Moses, and the message is one that burned in his heart after seeing the people whom he led forget God's goodness, resist His discipline, and live fruitless lives. In Psalm 90, Moses encourages us to "number our days aright, that we may gain a heart of wisdom," for "they quickly pass, and we fly away." How long do we have? We don't know. Yet Moses said that our life span would be, if we are blessed, seventy or eighty years. That's exactly what it is, on the statistical average, as we move into the twenty-first century. Now that I am in my fifties, that life span seems very, very short.

I don't want to be like the Israelites who wasted their lives because they failed to respond to God's discipline. When the peace and joy is gone from my life, I don't want to blame my circumstances, other people, or God. I want to look at myself, repent of my sin, and experience the fruit of the Spirit again. If I don't, I know God will keep me in the fire, because I am His heritage. That's what He did with Jacob.

For most of his life Jacob is the object of God's intense discipline. His home is a very unhappy home, and his heart is not one that sings. After twenty miserable years with a deceptive father-in-law and two battling wives, Jacob is ready (with a little prodding from God) to leave Haran with his families and return home. Again, he is in a tight spot. How will Esau receive him? Jacob remembers, "Oh yeah, God is my ally—I'll ask Him to help me." Bowing down before God, Jacob prays:

> *I am unworthy of all the kindness and faithfulness you have shown your servant. I had only my staff when I crossed this Jordan, but now I have become two groups. Save me, I pray, from the hand of my brother Esau, for I am afraid he will come and attack me, and also the mothers with their children.* (Genesis 32:10-11)

Is Jacob's repentance sincere? Or is he simply calling upon his ally from his foxhole once again? He goes on to remind God of His promise:

> *But you have said, 'I will surely make you prosper and will make your descendants like the sand of the sea, which cannot be counted.'* (Genesis 32:12)

WHEN WE ASK GOD FOR HELP, GOD PLANS THE AGENDA

Jacob sends five different herds or flocks ahead as a gift to warm Esau's heart. The messengers traveling with the flocks see Esau in the distance, coming with four hundred men! Running back, they inform Jacob of this distressing news and Jacob is terrified. *What are You doing, God?* he must have thought. But, as Psalm 115:3 tells us, "God does whatever pleases Him," and it pleased God to allow Jacob to be terrified.

And God is not done.

MUGGED BY AN ANGEL

That night, in his restless anxiety, Jacob sends his wives, their maidservants, and eleven sons across the Yabbok River without him. Dangerous, frightening—the whole scene feels like one from an eerie movie with ominous organ music playing in the background. Jacob paces alone on the bank of the river. *What is happening, God? Why aren't You answering my prayer the way I want You to answer it?* Suddenly Jacob is assaulted in the blackness. Can you imagine Jacob's thoughts? *What? Who is this? Esau?* All night long Jacob wrestled, and wrestled for his very life. Just when he thought he was finally winning, his assailant touched his hip and put it out of joint. Again, imagine Jacob's thoughts. *Oh! This is not Esau. This is an angel—or God Himself. My opponent has divine power.* At that point Jacob holds on, and will not let go, until he receives a blessing.

Do not miss the message here. We too wrestle with God. There have been times when I have lain awake at night and asked:

Lord, why is my dear friend Rita, a mother of two babies, dying? Why won't You spare her life?

Lord, I am in pain because of the strained relationship between me and a child. Won't You help me?

Why are You silent? Do You care?

When we are in pain, there are two possibilities. The first we must consider is that God is refining us, trying to purify us with His fire. The second is that there is no sin in our lives, but that God has a plan we cannot see, and we simply must trust Him. Charles Spurgeon said, "It will be profitable for any one of us who may be at this time out of conscious fellowship with the Lord, to inquire at His hands the reason for His anger, saying 'Shew me wherefore thou contendest with me?'"[5]

It took Jacob twenty years to face his sin, to realize that God wanted him to let go of his deceitful ways. During the wrestling match God makes Jacob tell Him his name. Why? Because the name Jacob means "deceiver or supplanter."

It has been a joy to have Billy Graham's youngest daughter, Ruth, at some of the Heritage Keepers conferences. What a wonderful heritage she has. Yet her brother, Franklin, was a prodigal for a number of years. His mother, Ruth, prayed:

> *Oh God of Jacob, who knew how to change supplanters then*
> *So deal, I pray, with this my son*
> *Though he may limp when Thou art done.*[6]

Wouldn't we rather our children limp into Glory than go whole somewhere else?

After Jacob owns His sin by saying His name, God changes his name to Israel, which means, "God rules." Finally, God was in charge of Jacob's life. Is Jacob changed? Yes. Though he still retains his Jacob nature, just as we will ever, on earth, retain our old nature, it is the new nature that prevails. Israel, unlike Jacob, is humble and penitent. His new character is evident the next morning:

> *He himself went on ahead and bowed down to the ground seven times as he approached his brother.* (Genesis 33:3)

The evidence that we are in the light is a song in our heart, a spring in our step, and the healing of relationships with others.

> *Esau ran to meet Jacob and embraced him; he threw his arms around his neck and kissed him. And they wept.* (Genesis 33:4)

God gave Jacob, as He will us, if we truly repent, songs of deliverance.

My Daughter, My Daughter

There is profound symbolism in God changing Jacob's name to Israel. In the mysterious way of God, Jacob—or Israel—represents both a man and the nation. You can see this in Hosea's prophecy:

> *The Lord has a charge to bring against Judah;*
> *he will punish Jacob according to his ways*
> *and repay him according to his deeds.*
> *In the womb he grasped his brother's heel;*
> *as a man he struggled with God.*
> *He struggled with the angel and overcame him;*
> *he wept and begged for his favor.*
> *He found him at Bethel and talked with him there—*
> *the Lord God Almighty, the Lord is his name of renown!*
> *But you must return to your God;*
> *maintain love and justice,*
> *and wait for your God always.* (Hosea 12:2-6)

About whom is Hosea speaking? A man or a country? It is both! The Scripture will often use the name of one of the early or famous ancestors to refer to a whole nation—God's chosen people, His heritage. The following passages from Hosea are some of my favorite Scriptures because they show the great tenderness God has for us, His children, despite our rebellion:

> *When Israel was a child, I loved him,*
> *and out of Egypt I called my son.*
> *But the more I called Israel,*
> *the further they went from me....*
>
> *It was I who taught Ephraim to walk,*
> *taking them by the arms;*
> *but they did not realize*
> *it was I who healed them.*
> *I led them with cords of human kindness,*
> *with ties of love;*
> *I lifted the yoke from their neck*
> *and bent down to feed them....*
> *How can I give you up, Ephraim?*
> *How can I hand you over, Israel?* (Excerpts from Hosea 11:1-8)

Like Jacob, you are His beloved and precious child. He knit you together in your mother's womb. He taught you to walk. He has a purpose for your life. He has watched over you all the days of your life, in your infancy, as an adolescent, and to today. If you are going your own way, it is breaking His heart. He is calling to you:

My daughter, My daughter

Will you hear? Will you respond? He hates to discipline you. He hates to hand you over to slavery and destruction and the consequences of not listening to Him—but He will if He must, for you are His *heritage.*

And if you step out on faith to serve Him, often, He will test you, to see if your faith is genuine. Often He will not come through until the last minute, so that you will trust in Him, and not in yourself.

THE NIGHT IS DARKEST BEFORE THE BREAK OF DAY

Bob and Lori and their families drove to the Heritage Keepers conference in Denver in a snowstorm. Fewer than three hundred women came. John Trent, Wellington Boone, and Marge Caldwell spoke to a basically empty auditorium. Financially, it was a disaster. They had to spend the Bowlings' retirement savings to pay the bills.

Two weeks later Lori flew to Indianapolis to do groundwork for the upcoming Heritage Keepers in September. The biggest church in Indianapolis would seat only 1,400. Lori knew Point of Grace would be with them—would that church be big enough? The only other alternative was Market Square Arena. Twenty thousand seats. Cavernous. God's answer? Or a tomb for Heritage Keepers?

Lori and Cindy Kardatzke, a member of the Heritage Keepers' praise team, met with prayer groups. Following the example of the Billy Graham Crusades and Promise Keepers, they began to pray in earnest with women in various churches and homes for the upcoming Heritage Keepers' Indianapolis Conference. Lori said:

It was one of the most spiritual weekends of my life. The presence of God was so real. I kept thinking about the book Experiencing God *and how it is important to find out where God is at work and join Him. I had this overwhelming sense that He was at work in Indianapolis.*

Lori walked through the rows of Market Square Arena. It was huge. The managers wanted to know: *Did she want to hold it for September 20?* Lori thought:

We have no money. We are in debt from Oklahoma City and Denver. If they ask for a deposit, then we can't do it. But maybe they won't ask for a deposit. No—that's crazy. I've been in the convention business. Of course they will ask for a deposit. But then, maybe, if God is leading us here, they won't.

Lori said, "Yes, we'd like to hold it." Then she held her breath. Nothing was said about a deposit as the manager wrote Heritage Keepers down for September 20. Lori called Bob.

Lori: "Bob, I've asked them to hold Market Square Arena for September twentieth."

Bob: "Lori, are you crazy?"

Lori: "I know, I know. But nothing was said about a deposit. If they ask for a deposit, well, then—we'll tell them we don't have it—but they aren't saying anything about a deposit."

Bob: "Lori, we can't even fill a church. Why in the world would you think we would have enough to go into an arena?"

Lori: "Bob, I just can't explain it. I sense the Spirit of God here so strongly."

Bob: "Come home, Lori—and we'll talk about it."

Men are called by God to be the providers for their families (1 Timothy 5:8), and Bob was feeling the weight of the debts. He didn't want to shrink back from God's will, but he was confused. As he waited for Lori to return, his thoughts flashed back to the first conference in Wichita when Coach Bill McCartney, who founded Promise Keepers, came to encourage them in this sister ministry. Looking for a private place to pray and encourage Bob, Coach McCartney led him down a side hall. Onlookers still were watching. The coach turned his back to them, knelt down, and took off his own shoes—first one, then the other. *What is he doing?* Bob wondered. Then the coach stood up and looked Bob in the eyes. "Remember, Bob. Ministry is never about the man who wears those shoes. It's always about what Christ is going to do through this ministry."

O Lord, Bob prayed. *Help me and my fears get out of the way. Give me discernment. Give Lori and me a like-mindedness in You.* When Lori came back, Bob listened to her with hearing ears. "Everything she was saying," Bob remembered, "was about prayer—about how God had spoken to her through prayer, and through the praying women in Indianapolis. She felt Jesus was going to do something in Indianapolis, and we needed to trust Him." Bob paced back and forth in their living room, his spirit crying out to God. Soon his anxious thoughts were replaced by an incredible peace.

Bob: *"Okay, Lori. We've gone this far—we might as well go the whole way."*

Lori: *"Market Square?"*

Bob smiled: *"Market Square!"*

If this is a success, Bob thought, *everyone will know it was God and not us—for this is way beyond us.*

MARKET SQUARE ARENA: SEPTEMBER 20, 1997

The manager of Market Square never asked for a deposit.

Heritage Keepers put minimal advertising into Indianapolis, but massive prayer.

Despite major summer thunderstorms delaying flights, all the speakers and singers arrived in time.

Eight thousand women came to this first engagement in Indianapolis.

Point of Grace sang their hearts out, and Denise did not go into labor. Heritage Keepers was the first large women's conference for Point of Grace, showing them how responsive women were to them. Following this, Point of Grace began singing for other women's conferences as well, including Women of Faith.

Hundreds of women went forward to receive Christ. Lives were changed. One woman who was planning to commit suicide that night, instead, gave her life to Christ and found her despair replaced with the steady beat of hope.

The Bowlings recouped their financial losses.

The God of Abraham, Isaac, and Jacob gave songs of deliverance. And He had only just begun.

Panning for Heritage Gold

☀ Icebreaker: Just as we hand down strengths to the next generation, we hand down weaknesses. Finish this sentence: I hope my children (or children of the next generation) don't

_____ the way I do.

1. What stood out to you from the text and Scriptures in the eighth chapter? Why?

The Jacob story is a page turner, better than the most fascinating fiction. Curl up with your Bible and read Genesis 25:19 through Genesis 35. Whenever you see Jacob being refined by God, highlight the passage or draw a flame in the margin.

☀ Read Genesis 28:10-22.

2. Describe Jacob's dream, vision, and the promises of God. Give verse references.

3. Describe Jacob's response with verse references.

4. Compare the following passages and record how God refined Jacob. What parallels do you see?

    A. Genesis 27:15-24 with Genesis 29:23-25

    B. Genesis 27:9 with Genesis 37:28-33

    C. Genesis 27:36 with Genesis 31:7

5. Share a time when God refined you by allowing you to experience the consequences of your own sin.

6. Think about a time when you were deeply hurt because of another's sin. As you think about that, do you see any tendency toward that same character flaw in yourself? (Share only if you choose, and if you do, do it carefully—not to hurt the one who hurt you, but to reveal what you learned about yourself.)

How do you think the refined Jacob might have answered the above question? What did he feel? What did he learn?

7. Are you going through pain right now? What could you learn from it?

8. Find similarities in the homes of Abraham and Isaac and then Isaac and Jacob. Compare

    A. Genesis 12:11-13 with Genesis 26:7

    B. Genesis 25:28 with Genesis 29:30 and 37:3

    C. Genesis 27:41 with Genesis 37:17-18

9. Philip Yancey says that either grace or ungrace is handed down through the generations. What did Rachel and Leah hand down? Give evidence.

10. Are you handing down grace? For example:

　　A. What kind of tone is present at your family supper table?

　　B. How do you react to a family member who has hurt you?

☼ Read Genesis 32:22-31.

11. Describe the setting, the assault, and the words spoken between Jacob and "the man."

12. Why do you think "the man" had Jacob tell Him his name? (For help, see Genesis 27:36.)

What significance do you see in Jacob's name being changed?

13. What are some of the things about which you wrestle with God? Are you willing to hold onto God, even in your pain, until you receive a blessing?

14. In Genesis 33:3-5, what evidence can you find for a refined Jacob?

Read Hosea 12:2-6.

15. What new insights does the prophet give you concerning God's dealings with Jacob and Jacob's response?

Read Hosea 11.

16. What emotions does God feel toward His heritage, His people—whether it is an individual or a nation? Give Scripture references.

17. What has God shown you through this lesson?

PRAYER TIME:

In groups of three, make yourself vulnerable to one another. Confess your sins. Share where you are in pain. Ask God for wisdom.

Nine

I'm turning forty next week and I may never have a child.
But the Lord revealed to me that through this song
('A Baby's Prayer') more babies have been born than
I could ever deliver through my womb.

KATHY TROCCOLI, WICHITA HERITAGE KEEPERS CONFERENCE:

JUNE 20, 1998

Kathy Troccoli: A Single Woman Passing on the Heritage

*Y*ou don't have to be a mother to give birth. I don't know if anyone demonstrates that better than Kathy Troccoli, whom Max Lucado describes as having "the heart of a missionary, the depth of a mystic, the joy of a child, and the voice of a Broadway singer."[1] Only God knows how many babies have been saved because of her pro-life song, "A Baby's Prayer." Only God knows how many souls have been saved because of her clear testimony on the saving power of Christ. And only God knows how many women have been revived to live a transformed life because of her winsome way. When Kathy ministered at her first Heritage Keepers conference you could almost hear the silence in the audience. She spoke from the heart:

> There's something about turning forty that makes me more sober than ever to the fact that I want to live for Him, I want to die for Him. I want to live an uncompromising life. I truly want to be a woman that when people meet me they would believe that Jesus existed because He was so powerful in me. I believe that's what true Christianity is about. I fail so much, but I want to be so filled with the river of life that it would just

*splash on people around me. That has been my prayer. That I would just
be a true reflection of Jesus' love.*

As I have had the privilege of getting to know Kathy, I have asked
myself what makes her life so fruitful. I long to be good ground,
the kind that Jesus says will produce thirty, sixty, or even a hundred
times what was sown. During our conversations, Kathy has been enor-
mously transparent with me, for that is her nature, and part of the
reason, I believe, God is using her so powerfully. Her friend Ellie told me:

*Her transparency makes women feel so close to her. One night when I was
having dinner with her at a nice restaurant, two women came up to her
and asked for prayer: one was facing a hysterectomy, another told her
things I wouldn't want you to put in print, and I'm looking at Kath, saying,
"Please pass the butter."*

Kathy amazed me when I boldly asked her for the names and
phone numbers of some of her closest friends so that I could interview
them. "Absolutely," she said generously, and started writing down their
names and numbers immediately. (I believe the insight from these
friends will be a feast for you, as it was for me.) Ellie, Allyson, and
Pamela are three of Kathy's dearest friends, her accountability
partners, and perennials in her life. Kathy asked, in her dauntless way,
"Perennial friend? *What* does that mean?"

Annuals are those friends whom God gives us for a season to
brighten our lives (or for us to brighten their lives) but then they fade
away and are gone. But now and then God will give us a perennial: the
kind of friend who is there season, after season, after season. I don't
think God gives us many perennials, though He may give a woman in
Kathy's circumstances more. (In many ways, Kathy walks this road
alone, for she has lost both parents to cancer, she has not married, and
she has not had children. We all need human support, but a person as
successful as Kathy faces enormous pressure and many temptations,
so God seems to have surrounded her with a generous supply of godly
women friends.)

In fact, after seeing the initial draft of this chapter, Kathy was concerned about excluding dear friends, and started naming them, "like Dorothy," she said, "who just accompanied me to my yearly mammogram." But for purposes of practicality, we limited my interviews to Ellie, Pamela, and Allyson. I was impressed with each of them, with their depth of insight, and especially with a God who understood exactly what Kathy needed. These three friends each love Kathy deeply, and their observations challenged me and often made me *think*, the way godly fellowship should.

One of the qualities all three friends saw in Kathy (though Kathy wasn't sure she was there yet) was that she was deeply in love with Jesus. Ellie put it like this:

I've seen Kathy fall more in love with Jesus through His constant, very real, very tangible reminders of His love for her. Just when she feels like she's blown it too many times, just when she feels like she really will never measure up, He always comes over her, always, always, always, like a gentle wave.

LET JESUS BE YOUR FIRST LOVE

Some of the Christian women I know who have a particularly deep walk are single women. Is there a connection? One of my single woman friends expressed it to me like this:

I come home to an empty apartment, the other side of my bed is empty, and I wake and have breakfast with no one on the other side of the table. With whom do I confide my inmost soul? With whom do I share my tears in the night? With whom do I go over my plans for the day? Jesus. Jesus. Jesus.

Pamela Muse manages some of the biggest names in Christian music, though not Kathy. Kathy lives with Pamela when she is in Nashville, and she has a study of her own in Pamela's home. I could tell how much that meant to Kathy when she called me from the road recently. Enthusiastically, she said, "I have a home in Nashville now!" Being a sojourner on earth has never been easy, even when it involves motels instead of tents. How wonderful to have not just a home, but a welcoming friend in that home. Pamela and Kathy give each other insight into their opposite hemispheres of manager and artist in the Christian music industry. I've been impressed that each of these women has been able to keep her feet on the ground in the midst of enormous success. Perhaps it is because they really have grasped, as Lori often says, that the ground is level at the cross. Pamela is also Kathy's dearest single friend, and that gives them yet another bond. I asked Pamela if she thought Kathy's singleness had augmented her relationship with Jesus. *Definitely*, Pamela said immediately. Reflectively, she explained:

> *Kath and I have talked about this forever. Jesus becomes not only her Savior, but Husband, Friend. It's a huge advantage for someone who is single. When the house or hotel room is quiet, it gives you a lot of time to really know His presence. If a married friend's husband goes away, she's trying to fill that void, because she isn't used to letting Jesus fill that void. But for Kathleen and me, that's our lives.*

Though some who are married might protest, saying they *do* let Jesus fill the void, I think many others would admit single women may have an edge here.

Kathy's songs are full of passion, expressing her intimacy with Jesus. A friend commented on her ballad, "When I Look at You," saying it was pretty bold to say: **Hold me, don't let me go, I need You** . . . in that really desperate, passionate way about God. Kathy responded:

> *But that's the way I live with Him! And that's the way I want to express my relationship with Him to the world—to help them understand that He's as close as our very breath, and we can get that close to Him.* [2]

Paul talks about the "divided" interests of the married:

> *An unmarried woman or virgin is concerned about the Lord's affairs: Her aim is to be devoted to the Lord in both body and spirit. But a married woman is concerned about the affairs of this world—how she can please her husband.* (1 Corinthians 7:34)

Pamela's words came back to me. It's a huge advantage to be single. We don't often look at it that way, because our vision is so earthbound, but if we could see into eternity, we might understand better. When Kathy shared with the Heritage Keepers' audience, I saw that passion in her to please the Lord—about which Paul talks. Earnestly, Kathy said:

> *I have absolutely broken God's heart. I also know He's been delighted in the times I've strived to be obedient and when I desire to do His will.*

Kathy feels His pleasure, like the smile of a lover. And because of her close relationship with Him, she is bearing much fruit. If you are a single woman and are thinking only a mother can pass on the heritage, think again. You may actually be *more* fruitful than a wife and mother. If you are clinging to Christ the way many of us cling to our husbands, you will bear fruit, and your garden is much bigger than your own backyard—it is the whole wide world.

What can we who are married learn from this? We must run to Jesus first, we must cling to Him, and we must ask Him to help us grow deeper and deeper in love with Him. Though we should cherish our husbands, Jesus should be our First Love.

Our tendency, especially as women because we are the relational sex, is to run to a human instead of to God with our joys and sorrows. Recently, when speaking in Dallas, I held a question-and-answer session. One young woman stood up and asked:

How can I know if God is first in my life?

It was a good question. I answered:

When you wake in the morning, do you run into His arms? Or do you put Him off, until the day has slipped away?

When you are troubled, do you run to Him—or do you run to the phone?

Do you long to stay in the light of His favor? And are you grieved when you walk into the darkness because you know you have hurt your First Love? Or do you see secret sins as better friends than Jesus?

Though I am not single, some of the times of greatest growth in my life occurred when my husband was so busy in his medical training that he simply did not have time for me, and we were simultaneously in a new town where I had neither family or friends. I believe God provided those desert times of human companionship for me so that my roots would stretch out to the Living Water.

This is how Kathy Troccoli and Pamela Muse have responded to their singleness, by sinking their roots deep into Jesus. Their lives are incredibly fruitful, and their garden is the whole wide world. Not only does Kathy nurture her fans, she seizes opportunities to nurture the children in her life: nieces and the children of her friends. Allyson Baker, Kathy's longest perennial friend, is the mother of three little boys. Kathy often stays with Allyson when she is traveling through Indiana. Allyson said:

Kathy gives so much to our children. She blesses them with a holy touch. She has holiness in her heart, and as she cuddles them, she dreams about their character, and prays for them. She tells them what she loves about them. She calls them on the telephone. She remembers them. When she prays for them, and she is faithful to do so, she knows how to pray because she knows their character. And she knows me and my sin structure—where I'm weak and where I'm strong.

Ellie Lofaro is Kathy's most colorful perennial friend and is the friend, Kathy says, who is most like her. When I was interviewing Ellie, I often felt as though I was talking to Kathy—and not just because they were Italians with a New York accent. Both made me laugh with their bold honesty, wry humor, and enthusiasm for life. Ellie has three children whom she has named after famous places: *Paris* (the city of light), *Jordan* (the river of life), and their youngest, *Capri* (the island of love). Ellie laughed and warned, "Once I started this, I couldn't continue on with a Debbie—Paris and Debbie just wouldn't work." (When I interviewed Ellie, who was so much fun, I heard water splashing on the other end of the phone. "What's going on?" I asked. "Capri is taking a bath," Ellie explained. *Appropriate*, I thought, *for an island*.) Ellie's children love Kathy, and Ellie is thankful for Kathy's input into their lives:

I love it that Paris, who will be a teenager next year, sees Kathy as a "cool" adult, and listens intently to Kathy about issues she will be facing in her teenage years.

Kathy loves children—in fact, Kathy loves people. If at all possible, she stays after her concerts for hours to hug and greet people. One of the ways she passes on the heritage is by being sensitive to anyone God brings across her path.

A little girl named Chelsea ran up to Kathy in the hall before a Heritage Keepers' conference. Breathlessly, Chelsea pulled out some pictures to show Kathy. Later, Kathy asked Chelsea to come up on stage. "Tell them what you told me," Kathy smiled, holding the mike up to Chelsea.

"I have a Corgi dog—and I named her Troccoli!" Kathy burst out in laughter and hugged Chelsea, who will never forget the moment, and who will, it is likely, grow up to love Jesus like her mentor.

You certainly don't have to be a mother to pass on the heritage and Kathy is living proof of that. For those of us who are mothers, the garden of our own children is immensely important and must not be neglected, but we must not limit our vision to them. God may be bringing others in desperate need of a drink of the Living Water into our garden: the friends of our children, our neighbors, and younger women in need of mentoring.

WALK IN YOUR ANOINTING

God has uniquely gifted each of us for a specific calling. We are going to be more fruitful in the areas where we have gifts, in the areas where we have seen we are effective, than in the areas where we are not gifted. When I sing, I produce *no* fruit. When I try to administer, I lose important lists. But when I speak, I see people respond. This is such an obvious principle, but I think we each need to pay careful attention to it so that we can redeem our fleeting days.

Pamela told Kathy to "walk in her anointing." I thought that was such an interesting phrase, one that could be helpful to each of us. In addition to considering your gifts and talents, Pamela said:

Anointing is when you are keeping pace with God. There is a wonderful era in your life when you've been through all the heartache and He's prepared you for your calling. All the machinery is working and the Holy Spirit is using you as a vessel. You're in step with the Lord, and there's an anointing that comes with that.

What has the heartache in Kathy's life birthed in her? Having lost both parents to cancer, having lost loves, and, perhaps, the opportunity to have children, she can identify with the pain of loss. I asked Allyson why she thought Kathy's life was so fruitful. As Allyson rocked her precious infant son, she said:

The first thing that comes to my mind is Romans 5, where Paul talks about the dominoes of character that suffering can produce: suffering produces perseverance; perseverance, character; and character, hope. Suffering can either undo you or push you to God. But Kath has leaned into her suffering in a very biblical sense, a Romans 5 sense, and it has produced tremendous character.

LEAN INTO YOUR SUFFERING

Even when Kathy was in her twenties, producer Brown Bannister described her as having "a breaking of the heart" ministry. But because she has leaned into her suffering in these last fifteen years, her life is more fruitful than ever. She has been willing to allow God to prune her, so she brings forth more fruit.

In Luci Shaw's book *Water My Soul*, she echoes the truth of the importance of leaning into your pain:

After the death of my husband, Harold, I learned an important lesson about my own pain, heart pain. I learned not to dodge it, not to try to distract myself from it, not to efface it with tranquilizers or busy-ness or mind games. I had to stay with the pain, to let that deep anguish hurt, because I sense it had a work to do in me.[3]

God allows pain in your life for a reason. Embrace your pain, "lean into it" with perseverance. Don't give up on God: hold on to Him, as Jacob did when he wrestled with Him in the night, and you will, eventually, be blessed. Pain can lead, if you persevere, to character, and then to hope. Kathy has wept many tears. Ellie said:

Kathy's cried more than anybody I've ever met. She will never get an ulcer from stuffing things! A few months ago, for no special occasion, she gave me a necklace with a little bottle on it. Then she showed me where David says: "You have collected all my tears and preserved them in your bottle!" (Psalm 56:8b TLB)

Kathy, in her pain, has experienced comfort from God. One of the purposes of pain is to pass on the comfort we have received to friends undergoing similar pain. Have you had a miscarriage? Have you had a family member die of cancer? Have you experienced a prodigal child? Whatever your pain, if God has comforted you, you are now equipped to pass on that heritage of comfort (2 Corinthians 1:3-4).

At a recent Heritage Keepers, Kathy sang her heartrending song "Good-Bye for Now," borne out of the pain of losing parents, and which, I am sure, is being sung at funerals everywhere. Beginning with her whispered, "I can't believe that you're really gone …" the song builds and swells to the hope we have in Christ of holding our loved ones again, of laughing with them, and of never saying good-bye again. As she sang, I watched boxes of Kleenex, literally, being passed down the rows, as women wept unabashedly. Halfway through the song the women stood up, clapping and crying. Kathy reflected on that moment: "I specifically knew in my spirit, when they stood up, it wasn't that I was singing this powerhouse ballad and my voice was so great. At that moment I felt the women were saying: *Yes! I'll see my loved ones again. Thank you for reminding me. Yes!* That made me feel good because that's what I'm trying to do with my music. It's not about me. It's about the message and how it can bring you life."

Kathy is embracing her holy heritage, the great riches she has in Christ, and she is passing them on to others. We can do the same.

EXPRESS YOUR FEMININE SOUL

Kathy is a kindred spirit with the female soul. When Kathy comes out at women's conferences she says: I love, love, love singing to women. I asked her why. She said:

Well, I think it's about the way women are made. Women are so receptive—so in touch with their emotions. They're able to get vulnerable in a second. A lot of these women are mothers and they're getting out of the house and it's their time with their friends and they're so, so there— and they want to be there with their whole heart. They not only want to have a party time because they're out, but a lot of these women are coming in, like the woman in Luke's Gospel with the issue of blood, profusely bleeding. There's a lot more of the inhibitions down, the walls down. . . . It's the difference between going out to dinner with my friends when they're with their husbands or going to dinner with my friends when they're by themselves—there's a different girl-thing that happens.

When I asked Allyson why she thought Kathy had such a huge appeal to women. She said:

God has created the soul of a man to reflect a masculinity and the soul of a woman to reflect a femininity. Kathy is very distinctively feminine. The way she carries herself, the way she invites others in and nurtures them, and even her songwriting calls out the feminine heart: the big ballads, the love songs, the transparency of her lyrics, the sweetness of her themes. Her presentation and her voice are vulnerable, feminine, and nurturing.

(Kathy protested, as she has always felt like a tomboy. "Sheila Walsh—Terry Meeuwsen—that's feminine." But Allyson stood firm on her quote.) Kathy's New York boldness is not what we traditionally associate with femininity. Once she began a phone conversation with me by saying, "I found a terrible sentence in your manuscript!" ("Hey!" I exclaimed, clutching my wounded writer's pride.) But the honesty she directs at you she also directs at herself, revealing the transparency of the female soul, which can cut through layers of pretense like an X-acto knife. Ellie said:

> *I have never ever ever been to a concert where she doesn't say, "Kathy Troccoli is a sinner." When Kathy is done stripping herself down, being naked and honest, weeping about what a wretched woman she is in front of stadiums of fifteen to twenty thousand women, I have to think: "How dare I be masked or aloof? How dare I be too proud to be truthful?"*
>
> *We are so adept in the Christian culture of pretension and of communicating lies. But we reap what we sow. Kathy's honesty, a model to us all, is reaping much fruit.*

I would encourage you, when you are with good friends, when you are sharing in a small group, to be transparent with one another. I have learned that the more transparent I am, the more I can minister and release transparency in others. When I confess that I was afraid to adopt a child with a missing arm because I was concerned about appearances, people are at first aghast, but then they listen. I tell them how selfish and shallow I was. I explain how God had to prune me. When I admit my sin, my selfishness, and my pride—people connect, for they have sin natures as well. I can be a catalyst in a friendship or in a small group, helping others be honest. When I share where I am *still* struggling, such as in being judgmental, or in running to food instead of to God for comfort, I get the kind of prayer support I desperately need. God encourages us to confess our sins to one another, so that we might be healed. (James 5:16) Why pretend? Life is too short and eternity too long for playing games.

When Lori introduced Kathy with accolades at the first Heritage Keepers, Kathy said, *Give me more, more* and we all laughed—for we loved her humanness, knowing how our own hearts long for praise. I believe we can move into a deeper walk with each other and with God by embracing and expressing the vulnerability of our female souls.

Kathy's first women's conference was Time Out for Women, and the response gave her a taste of her future. For five solid hours afterward she autographed, hugged, and ministered to women. She sold two thousand copies of her book, *My Life Is in Your Hands*. During those five hours she felt she had a glimpse of her future, her call to women. She remembered something Pamela told her:

> *You're different, Kathy. You aren't going to just sing your song, get on a bus, and sing to churches. God is going to take you down a different road. I think it's going to be a healing ministry—maybe heart healing, soul healing.*

The Holy Spirit is using Kathy as a vehicle to speak healing to people. She has done it for me, in part, by expressing her nurturing side. When I came to her concert, she acknowledged me to the audience and walked down to where I was seated. When I stood she kissed my cheek, and thanked me for not writing what she calls *Christianity lite*. She was not afraid to hug me, to nurture me—and it was like spring rain to my soul.

AN UNSEEN HAND GUIDING US

A week after the first Heritage Keepers conference in Indianapolis, Lori Beckler was vacuuming with her CD player on, the volume turned high, so she could hear the music over the drone of her Hoover. When Kathy Troccoli's "Go Light Your World" came on, Lori paused, visualizing the women coming forward at the Indianapolis conference. *How perfect that song would be for closing the conferences*, Lori thought. *That's what Heritage Keepers is all about, passing on His light to the world, to the next generation, the light spreading and spreading—diffusing the darkness. Oh my goodness, I'd love to have our praise team close next year's Indianapolis conference with "Go Light Your World."* Lori turned off the vacuum, wrapped the cord around the handle hooks, and put it in the closet humming the melody. She went over and pressed the replay button and curled up in an overstuffed chair, closed her eyes, and visualized the women coming forward. Lori said:

> *It didn't even occur to me that we might invite Kathy to come: I guess I*

wasn't thinking that big. And though I loved Kathy's music—I didn't know anything about the woman, Kathy Troccoli. But I knew when we had our closing finale—it had to be: "Go Light Your World."

Two months later, Lori and her friends Cindy Baldwin and Trish Pickard drove to Dallas for the national prayer and fasting conference from Wednesday to Friday noon. I find this timing intriguing, because it seems God often breaks through after an earnest time of seeking His face through prayer and fasting. When Esther and her maids, for example, prayed and fasted for three days, they then saw God on the move.

Lori had planned to arrive back in Wichita for a Friday night concert, feeling it would be a perfect way to close her three-day fast. Providentially, it was a Kathy Troccoli concert. Lori explained:

> *I had no intentions of meeting Kathy—I wasn't thinking that we could bring her to Heritage Keepers. I was purely thinking of my own personal enrichment, and of worshiping the Lord in this way at the close of my fast. My family and friends had other commitments, so I went all by myself. I slid in and I slid out. The concert was absolutely wonderful, and so glorifying to God.*

After the concert, Kathy was signing autographs. Cheryl Hurley, who books concerts in Wichita, was standing nearby, visiting with a friend of Kathy's. Kathy heard Cheryl mention Heritage Keepers and her ears perked up. Kathy recalled the moment:

> *I had read about Heritage Keepers somewhere and I liked the name. And I had this sense that God was calling me to do women's conferences. So, I told Cheryl I'd really like to talk to the woman setting up the Heritage Keepers conferences.*

Those familiar with the world of well-known Christian artists will know how unusual this interaction was. Kathy's bookings are done by the William Morris Agency. She *does not* initiate bookings. She told me:

> *I never do that. I mean, it seems presumptuous to tell someone you are supposed to sing at their conference—but, I felt compelled.*

The next day Kathy called Lori from her motel room. *Lori*, she said, *this is Kathy Troccoli*. Surprised, Lori sat down and listened.

This is really odd for me, but would you consider having me—I mean—I know you have some people on your program and it's all set, 'cause I know they book them so far in advance—I have sixteen next year, going into November '99, but, if the dates would work, would you consider having me at your conferences?

I asked, "Well, did Lori say, *Yes! Yes! Yes!*"? Kathy shook her head and laughed her deep throaty laugh.

She said how excited she was that I'd called, and we visited for nearly forty-five minutes. She asked me where my heart was—and I sensed this connection with her as we talked. I loved it that she didn't immediately ask me to come. She wanted to take it to the board, to prayer, and then she asked me to pray about it for a week.

But then, all of a sudden, she burst out: "Wouldn't it be amazing to have you close the conference with 'Go Light Your World'?"

I smiled, knowing Lori. She tries to be cautious and wise, but her enthusiasm can leap out like a malfunctioning jack-in-the-box.

Kathy's response was warm and generous. She said: "Even if I just came for that—I'd come and close your conference with 'Go Light Your World.'"

One of the things I have seen in Kathy that is a model to us all, no matter our ministry, is that her life is not about exalting herself but about exalting Christ. She was willing to travel to a Heritage Keepers' conference to sing just one song if that's what God wanted her to do.

In less than a week Lori called back. Both were convinced that God was leading Kathy to be a part of Heritage Keepers. At the next conference, Kathy gave a miniconcert, to which the women responded profoundly. When she closed with "Go Light Your World," the presence of the Lord was so real, so strong. You had the sense that though this was a mountain-top high, that it wasn't just an emotional high. The women *were* going to carry the light down the mountain and into the valley, into their homes, their community—so that the next generation would know, even the children yet to be born.

When you consider that each woman at a Heritage Keepers conference represents family, friends, and generations to come, you begin to picture a sea of people spreading out beyond where the eye can see.

THEY WERE FRUITFUL, AND MULTIPLIED GREATLY

The heartbeat of Heritage Keepers is that God is concerned with much more than just our generation, for He sees the generations to come. A hidden truth emerges as you look at some of the repeated word pictures given from Genesis to Revelation. One God uses is the stars, as when He showed Abraham the stars and said, "So shall your offspring be." (Genesis 15:5b) Another word God often uses is *teeming*. It is translated in different ways from the Hebrew, but God uses it, creatively, to describe the teeming fish He made at Creation, the teeming frogs He caused to multiply during the plagues, and the teeming people, who are *His heritage*. There is a message here, a message God longs for you to understand.

Pictures often stay in our memory better than words, so imagine the pictures these words paint. The first has to do with "teeming fish in the sea."

There is the sea, vast and spacious, teeming with creatures beyond number. (Psalm 104:25)

As a little girl I would lie on my belly on a pier sticking into Green Bay and watch, in wonder, as thousands of minnows swam beneath me. Once in my life I have convinced my husband to snorkel with me in Hawaii. (When we returned I said the highlight of my trip was actually seeing, firsthand, the teeming swarms of yellow, red, and polka-dotted fish. My husband said *his* highlight was not drowning.)

Another picture, but a less beautiful one, is that of the teeming frogs and swarming flies God used as part of the plagues in Egypt.

The Nile will teem with frogs. They will come up into your palace and your bedroom and onto your bed, into the houses of your officials and on your people, and into your ovens and kneading troughs. (Exodus 8:3)

If you do not let my people go, I will send swarms of flies on you and your officials, on your people and into your houses. The houses of the Egyptians will be full of flies, and even the ground where they are. (Exodus 8:21)

It is interesting to discover that the very same Hebrew phrases used to describe swarms of animal life are used to describe the enormous multitude of people who descended from Jacob in Exodus 1:7:

But the Israelites were fruitful and multiplied greatly and became exceedingly numerous, so that the land was filled with them.

It doesn't stop here. The Bible fits together from Genesis to Revelation. From Abraham would come a teeming multitude. We saw it being fulfilled in the very opening of Exodus, when the teeming people of God were a problem to the Egyptians. But they continue to multiply, for no matter what the Pharaoh tries, God's plan cannot be stopped. Exodus begins, simply, with a list of names, the names of the sons of Jacob. Jacob's twelve sons quickly turned to seventy descendants, and from the seventy, came a *nation*.

The parallel is repeated in the Gospels. Jesus had twelve disciples. By the time we get to the tenth chapter of Luke, there are seventy. From those seventy came all of Christendom, including you and me, if we have put our trust in Christ. Beyond us is a multitude that no man can count. This spectacular scene that is hinted at in Genesis comes to fruition in Revelation 7: 4-10. After John lists the tribes of Israel, each tribe numbering twelve thousand, the apostle turns and breathlessly describes his vision:

After this I looked and there before me was a great multitude that no one could count, from every nation, tribe, people and language, standing before the throne and in front of the Lamb. They were wearing white robes and were holding palm branches in their hands. And they cried out in a loud voice: "Salvation belongs to our God, who sits on the throne, and to the Lamb."

In writing this book I have had the sense that this message of *being the heritage of God* is much bigger than I or anyone at Heritage Keepers realized. God cares about His people, about me and you, not only because He loves us individually, but because He looks ahead to the multitude that no one can count. No wonder He calls:

My daughter, My daughter
My precious child,
Embrace your holy heritage
So that the next generation will know

GO LIGHT YOUR WORLD

I like the way Kathy Troccoli expressed it to me as I listened to her in her crowded little dressing room, as she was applying her makeup before a concert:

In the little time I have on stage, I want to be able to fill some of the empty and worn buckets with God's light.

In the same way, God calls us, as His daughters, in the little time we have on the stage of life, to pass His light to the people He puts in our path. How do we pass the light? The same way Sarah did. Remember? *She did what was right and she did not give way to fear.* (1 Peter 3:6) This is the model of the holy women of old: Sarah, the Hebrew midwives, Jochebed, and others. These holy ancestors are our models, our heritage. If, every day, *we would do what was right and not give way to fear*, we *would* pass His light to the world.

A BABY'S PRAYER

I'll never forget hearing Kathy sing "A Baby's Prayer" at Heritage Keepers. She prefaced it with her usual bold honesty, yet her incredible compassion for the women who had committed the sin of abortion and were caught in a prison of guilt:

Amazing things have been happening with this next song. I think it would be a sin not to sing it for you women. I have an incredible heart for the unborn and [her voice becomes strong and bold] *I believe partial birth abortion is straight from the pit of hell* [deafening applause] *and I will proclaim this across the nation.*

[Her voice grows tender.] *One out of every five women has had an abortion. Some of you are here. I sing this song for you. I have not had an abortion, but if we had time to share I would share the prisons God has freed me from and continues to free me from. I'm not all there yet—I'm still caged in some of them—but I pray that He'll set me free....We have an extraordinary God who does extraordinary things....So here it is for you, called "A Baby's Prayer."*

Then, on a dark stage, this beautiful Italian woman sits on a stool in a circle of light and gently sings:

I can hear her talking with a friend
I think it's all about me
Oh, how she can't have a baby now
My mommy doesn't see.
That I feel her breathe
I know her voice
Her blood it flows through my heart
God, you know my greatest wish is that
We'd never be apart....[4]

The song goes on to express love and forgiveness to the mothers who have made that fatal choice, and to assure them that their babies are in heaven with Jesus. Kathy told me an amazing story that occurred when she was singing "A Baby's Prayer" at a smaller women's conference.

There were about two thousand women present. As I was singing, a woman just came right up in the middle of the song, fell on her knees, and her head was even with the middle of my thigh. Silently I prayed, as I was singing: O God, give me Your heart. Well, she started a caravan of women;

they just started to stream toward me and kneel down, weeping. There must have been seventy-five women weeping and wailing. Thank God there were women from a post-abortive ministry there. As I was singing, I motioned to them to be ready to minister and I cried out in my spirit to God: Please give me the prayer, dear Lord, to release them. And He did. He gave me a prayer to grant them freedom, to reassure them that their babies were in heaven, to deliver them from shame and the guilt, to remind them that He throws our sins as far as the east is from the west and He remembers them no more. I told them: "You're remembering it and He doesn't want you to—except that you'll see your baby again."

How many women who have had abortions have experienced healing and new life because of Kathy's ministry? How many women who *might* have had abortions have reconsidered because of Kathy's ministry? Kathy tells about one such woman in her book *My Life Is in Your Hands.* On a return engagement to Oregon, a young woman approached Kathy after everyone had left:

Kathy, I had to wait to speak with you. You were here four years ago and spoke out for the unborn.... I was going to have an abortion that week. I want to thank you for what you said that night.

As she spoke, a precious little girl looked into Kathy's eyes. Her mother knelt down and drew her daughter close. *This is my little miracle.*[5]

Kathy is a true daughter of Sarah. She is *doing what is right* by speaking out against the evil of abortion, and she is doing it with the compassion, love, and humility of Christ. She *is not giving way to fear,* despite persecution from the press and the pro-choice movement. She fears only God. How like the Hebrew midwives!

THE HEBREW MIDWIVES

As the Israelites were fruitful and multiplied greatly, the Egyptians grew concerned. The contrast is stark: instead of *doing what is right and not giving way to fear,* the Egyptians do the exact opposite.

Their fear is the fear of man, whom Isaiah and Peter tell us not to fear. There seems to be little fear of God, however, for the Pharaoh's "Plan A" is to "deal shrewdly with them" by putting slave masters over them to oppress them and to lead, through harshness, to the deaths of the weaker Israelites. But the Pharaoh's plan was foiled, for the more the Israelites were oppressed, the more they multiplied. On to "Plan B":

> *The king of Egypt said to the Hebrew midwives, whose names were Shiphrah and Puah, "When you help the Hebrew women in childbirth and observe them on the delivery stool, if it is a boy, kill him; but if it is a girl, let her live."* (Exodus 1:15-16)

Why does everyone name their daughters Rachel and Leah—why not Shiphrah and Puah? (I'm just kidding. I don't really want a future innocent granddaughter to be named Puah.) Shiphrah and Puah certainly showed a strength of character, revealing themselves to be true daughters of Sarah:

> *The midwives, however, feared God and did not do what the king of Egypt had told them to do; they let the boys live.* (Exodus 1:17)

The king is furious. He summons them, glowering down at them, and rages:

> *Why have you done this? Why have you let the boys live?* (Exodus 1:18b)

What the Pharaoh does not realize is that he is opposing God. These are God's people, His heritage. God promised Abraham, Isaac, and Jacob that His heritage was going to be as numerous as the stars—and no one can stop God's covenant. The Hebrew midwives had a heart for these babies, and a fear of God, so they were able to stand firm. Their reply is a clever one, and pointed out the striking contrast between the indolent Egyptian women and the industrious Israelite women:

> *The midwives answered Pharaoh, "Hebrew women are not like Egyptian women; they are vigorous and give birth before the midwives arrive."* (Exodus 1:19)

George Rawlinson said the midwives were religious enough to avoid the shedding of innocent blood, but not so religious that they were willing to be martyred, so they resorted to deceit.[6] But God was pleased with them, and with their courageous stand, for we are told:

> *So God was kind to the midwives and the people increased and became even more numerous. And because the midwives feared God, he gave them families of their own.* (Exodus 1:20-21)

I have wondered if God will likewise bless Kathy Troccoli with a family of her own. She showed me the journal she is writing to her future husband—whoever he may be—for her heart's desire is to be married.

But, oh, how God is using her as a single woman.

A HERITAGE OF GRACE OR UNGRACE

Just as we are called to pass on the truths of God, we are called to pass on His grace. In *What's So Amazing about Grace*, Philip Yancey says that generations either pass down grace or ungrace.

Though God has given great grace to us, though "time after time" He has restrained His anger because "He remembered" we are "but flesh" (from Psalm 78:38-39), we often have trouble showing the same kind of grace to one another.

When Heritage Keepers invited Sandi Patty to come on board, not everyone agreed with the decision. After all, Sandi had committed adultery and divorced her husband. Yes, she was repentant. Yes, she confessed her sin. Yes, she dropped out of ministry for two years for a time of restoration. But should she sing to a vast audience like Heritage Keepers?

Whether or not you agree with the decision Heritage Keepers made, I'd like to share with you how they came to it, and to have you consider the impact of giving grace or ungrace to others and to the next generation.

Panning for Heritage Gold

☀ Icebreaker: Think about a ministry in which you have experienced fruitfulness, for this may help you discover your spiritual gifts and your "anointing." Share what it was in a few words. (This icebreaker could be expanded over a group meal where you would respond to one another.)

1. Explain what stood out to you from the text and Scriptures in this chapter concerning:

Letting Jesus be your first love

Walking in your anointing

Leaning into your suffering

Expressing your feminine soul

2. Now, make yourself vulnerable by writing down an area where you are struggling to obey God. Would you be willing to share this with the small group or with one trusted friend?

☀ Read Exodus 1. Highlight the three ways the Pharaoh tried to stem the fruitfulness of the Israelites.

3. Find all the phrases in Exodus 1:7 that record the fruitfulness of the Israelites.

How does Israel's fruitfulness correspond with the promises God made to Abraham, Isaac, and Jacob?

4. How did the new king use fear to motivate the Egyptians? What evidence can you find that his propaganda campaign was successful? (Exodus 1:9-14) List Scripture references.

What impact did the persecution have on fruitfulness? (v. 12)

5. What was Pharaoh's "Plan B"? (Exodus 1:15-16)

Put yourself in the place of the Hebrew midwives. What do you think your thoughts would be? Your feelings?

6. Describe how the midwives responded to the Pharaoh. (vv. 17-19)

7. How do the Hebrew midwives show themselves to be true daughters of Sarah? (See 1 Peter 3:6.)

When Peter tells us not to give way to fear, he quotes from Isaiah 8:12-13. Whom are we not to fear? Whom are we to fear? Why?

Whom did the Egyptians fear? Whom did they not fear?

8. How does God respond to the Hebrew midwives? (Exodus 1:20-21)

9. Apparently, up to this point, the Hebrew midwives did not have families of their own. Why might a single woman have a closer relationship to God than a married woman? What might you learn from this?

10. List a situation in your life right now where you need to do what is right and not give way to fear.

How can the above story from Exodus strengthen you to do this?

11. Why could the fruitfulness of the Israelites not be stemmed?

12. What parallel do you see in the following passages?

Exodus 1:2-5 _____ Luke 6:13 and Luke 10:1

Exodus 1:7 _____ Revelation 7:4-9.

☀ Read John 15:1-8.

13. Describe the word picture given.

14. What does Jesus say about the following?

    A. The true vine? (v. 1)

    B. The gardener? (v. 1)

    C. Branches that bear no fruit? (v. 2)

    D. Branches that bear fruit? (v. 2)

15. The Greek word for "prunes" also means "cleans." List a time when:

    A. The consequences of your sin caused pain and then repentance:

    B. God allowed pain into your life and you responded by clinging more closely to the vine:

16. What is the primary secret to bearing fruit? (vv. 4-5)

List every way you can think of to abide in Christ personally.

17. What is one condition of effective prayer? (v. 7)

18. Who is glorified when we bear fruit? (v. 8) Why?

19. What stands out to you from this lesson? How will you apply it to your life?

PRAYER TIME:

Pray in pairs concerning your answer to the last question.

Ten

Ungrace does its work quietly and lethally, like a poisonous,
undetectable gas. A father dies unforgiven.
A mother who once carried a child in her own body does
not speak to that child for half its life.
The toxin steals on, from generation to generation.[1]

PHILIP YANCEY

WHAT'S SO AMAZING ABOUT GRACE

Sandi Patty: Passing
on a Heritage of Grace

After Sandi Patty's divorce, she married Don Peslis, a fitness instructor who had toured with her as one of her backup singers. People were whispering. *Was it true? Had Sandi had an affair?* Less than two weeks after her marriage in 1995, she confessed her sin before her church and the Christian public. In an extensive interview with *Christianity Today,* she admitted her sexual immorality and her failure to be honest about it.

Another Christian artist fallen. She was our darling, and we were so proud of her, the recipient of thirty-five Dove Awards. Even the secular world recognized her talent. When she sang "The Star-Spangled Banner" on the Fourth of July in 1986, the phone lines were jammed at ABC News. Who was this soaring voice who sang the national anthem as it was meant to be sung?

For two years after her confession Sandi dropped out of the Christian music world. She received counseling, nourishment through an accountability group, Bible study, and prayer. Slowly, she began to experience signs of healing to a life ravaged by sinful choices. She and Don worked on blending their seven children and even went on to adopt a baby. But would she sing again to vast audiences? Would Christian radio play her music again? Would she *minister* with her talent—or had the anointing of God been snuffed out?

Heritage Keepers was one of the first groups to offer her the opportunity to return to ministry, and she came to the Wichita conference in 1998. Before I tell you why Bob and Lori felt led to offer her grace and an opportunity to minister again, I'd like to share with you a parallel I see in Scripture, for I think it may give you compassion and perspective.

MIRIAM, RAISED IN A GODLY HOME

We remember her as the sister standing guard over her baby brother's basket as it bobbed along the Nile. Miriam is a favorite of children's illustrators: a brave, obedient, and faithful big sister. Miriam certainly had a godly heritage. The faith of her parents is mentioned in the Hebrews Hall of Fame:

By faith Moses' parents hid him for three months after he was born, because they saw he was no ordinary child, and they were not afraid of the king's edict. (Hebrews 11:23)

Imagine being pregnant at a time when an edict had been given that all the male babies were to be thrown into the Nile to the crocodiles. Did Moses' mother, Jochebed, hope she was carrying a baby girl? Oh, I think so.

But Jochebed gave birth to a lusty baby boy. Imagine her feelings as she held her newborn son: so precious, so innocent, so vulnerable. What fear must have penetrated her heart! Yet, as a true daughter of Sarah, she does not give way to that fear, but, in faith, hides Moses for three months. How did she do it? How did she keep him from crying as soldiers prowled?

Did Jochebed teach Miriam to rock Moses in a hidden corner with honey on her thumb? Did she tell her daughter to pray, and to trust in God? Oh, I think so.

Did Jochebed involve Miriam in the creation of the "ark" to save her baby brother? As they daubed it together with pitch to seal out the water did she tell her daughter to pray, and to plead for God's mercy? Oh, I think so.

Did Jochebed rehearse with Miriam her speech if God answered their prayers and the daughter of the Pharaoh found Moses and had pity on him? Did she tell her daughter to pray for courage, and to trust in God's goodness?

Jennie Dimkoff is the younger sister of Heritage Keepers' speaker Carol Kent. Jennie is a talented speaker too and has helped me to identify with Jochobed. Jennie imagines the morning when Jochebed put her baby in the Nile:

> *She holds Moses one last time, feeling the velvet softness of his face in her neck, and her heart hurts. She puts him in the basket and covers him carefully. She hitches up her skirt in her waistband, picks up that basket on her hip, and steps into the reeds while Miriam, with pounding heart, watches. Then Jochebed comes back on shore and faces a little girl, saying: "Remember everything we practiced honey ... I love you so—Oh, don't be afraid Miriam—God is with you."...And then she does the hardest thing in her life. She walks away from her two vulnerable children and leaves them in God's hands.*[2]

The Heritage Keepers' psalm, Psalm 78, lists many of the miracles of Exodus, these miracles we are to teach to our children so that they can put their hope in God. Until recently I thought the Exodus miracles mentioned in Psalm 78 included only the plagues that God performed through the adult Moses and skipped over the early miracles, which involved the women (the Hebrew midwives, Jochebed, and the princess). Yet I felt led to include these miracles in *My Daughter, My Daughter*. Recently, I read in the *Pulpit Commentary: Exodus*, that the probable locality on the Nile where the princess came down from the palace to discover the infant Moses was "the region of Zoan." And then my heart burned within me as George Rawlinson referred to Psalm 78:12.[3]

> *He did miracles in the sight of their fathers in the land of Egypt, in the region of Zoan.*

Once again, I had the sense of God's strong hand pulling the *Heritage Keepers'* raft along the river, the river of Psalm 78. Once again I sensed His call:

> *My daughter, My daughter*
> *embrace your holy heritage*
> *so the next generation will know,*
> *even the children yet to be born.*

The young Miriam watched from behind the reeds to see what would happen to her baby brother. There, in the "region of Zoan," she witnessed a miracle. Soon the princess, the one woman in all of Egypt who could save Moses, came down the steps of the palace to bathe in the Nile River. Miriam held her breath as the princess spotted the basket and sent a slave girl out into the Nile to retrieve it. (I would not have wanted to wade out into those crocodile-infested waters! I can almost hear the theme music from *Jaws*.) When the princess opened the basket to discover a crying baby she immediately understood what desperation had driven a mother to do this, for she says, "This is one of the Hebrew babies." (Exodus 2:6) How did she know this? George Rawlinson says, "it is the way of woman" to be so intuitive, to know, quickly, what would have driven a mother to expose her baby like this.[4] I can imagine the racing thoughts of the princess: *No Egyptian woman would do this—but a Hebrew woman—because of my father's cruelty—yes— she would be driven to do this. Oh my—how can I let this beautiful baby die?* And so the princess decided, in a moment of compassion, to secretly defy her own father, the Pharaoh.

Then Miriam took a deep breath and stepped out from behind the reeds and said: "Shall I go and get one of the Hebrew women to nurse the baby for you?" (Exodus 2:7)

The princess responded: "Yes, go." Can't you picture Miriam racing along the riverbank and through the streets, all the while weeping tears of joy? When she arrived at the place where her mother was carrying bricks, were the Egyptian slavemasters watching, listening? Did they see the excitement in Miriam's eyes? Did they hear her say:

Mother! The princess has called for you! She wants—your help! She wants you right now!

Jochebed must have been delirious with joy: she would hold her baby again! And how awed she must have been by this confirmation that they belonged to a God who was mindful of them, who bent down and answered their prayers. He heard their groanings. He cared about their sufferings.

When Jochebed and Miriam arrived at the steps of the palace, the princess returned Moses to Jochebed's arms, and ordered: "Take this baby and nurse him for me, and I will pay you." (Exodus 2:9)

The life of her brother has been saved, and her mother has been given a reprieve: a few precious years to train Moses, to love him, and to help him know his heritage. And then, again in faith, she will let him go, returning him, as promised, to the arms of the Pharaoh's daughter.

This is the heritage that blessed Miriam.

SANDI, RAISED IN A GODLY HOME

At one Heritage Keepers I spoke about "Passing on a Heritage More Precious Than Silver." Afterward I asked the women to huddle in groups of three and share one truth a mentor or a mother had given to them that they were passing on to the next generation. Lori asked Sandi to "prime the pump," to give an example to the audience. Sandi gave a tribute to her mother:

*Instead of just saying "I love you," my mother would often say, "I love you **today**," meaning that though she loved us always and forever, we could also go off to school wrapped in the assurance that she was thinking of us, praying for us, and loving us **today**. I say the same thing to my children.*

Sandi gives a tribute to her dad in a letter she wrote to him on Father's Day in 1990, which is published in Gloria Gaither's book *What My Parents Did Right*. With great tenderness she writes to a man she still calls Daddy, and thanks him for the tremendous love he has shown her, her mother, and the whole family.[5]

I met Sandi Patty's parents years ago when they provided the music at a retreat where I was the speaker. (Sandi inherited amazing musical genes from both sides!) Her dad told a story of a time when God saved the life of Sandi's brother, Craig.

> It was a foggy, foggy morning in Indiana, and Craig was driving from one studio to another when there was a seven-car pile-up and the last vehicle was a semi. Though Craig was going very slowly, by the time he saw it, he slammed into the side of the semi. When we rushed to his side at the hospital, he was in a coma. It was a terrible time.
>
> After Craig had been in a coma for two months, Anna, who is Sandi's daughter, and who was just a toddler at the time, woke up in the morning saying, "Yea, Uncle Craig! Yea, Uncle Craig!"
>
> Sandi went in and said, "Honey, what are you saying?"
>
> "Yea, Uncle Craig! He's awake!"
>
> Sandi said, "How do you know that?" Bright-eyed Anna said, confidently, "Jesus told me!"

And yes, Jesus had indeed called to Anna, telling her that her Uncle Craig was waking up, for that was the day when Craig began to awaken and to return to health.

Like Miriam, Sandi saw God reach down and save her brother's life. Like Miriam, she experienced love and faith in her family. This is the heritage that blessed Sandi.

Yet Both Miriam and Sandi Experienced Pain in Childhood

Were the childhoods of Miriam and Sandi painless? Hardly. Miriam and her parents were slaves, abused by the Egyptians:

They made their lives bitter with hard labor in brick and mortar and with all kinds of work in the fields; in all their hard labor the Egyptians used them ruthlessly. (Exodus 1:14)

Though a godly family can give you strength to deal with the wounds a sin-sick world inflicts, it cannot always protect you from receiving those wounds. What kind of scars did being in bondage leave on Miriam? I would expect she had feelings of degradation, worthlessness, and self-hatred.

Sandi's family had its own heartaches and struggles as well. A family friend abused Sandi sexually when Sandi was six. The impact of a devastation like that is enormous, as those who are involved with counseling victims of childhood sexual abuse realize. Though you cannot see the victim's chains, they are as real as the chains that bind slaves. Typically, these victims have feelings of degradation, worthlessness, and self-hatred.

Sandi had those feelings, but she didn't know why. Sandi's marriage was strained. The pain in her marriage led her to Bible Study Fellowship, where she did the whole series. During that time a woman came to her one day and gave her a book called *God's Crippled Children*, saying, "Sandi, it's really been laid on my heart to give you this book." It was a book about childhood sexual abuse and the characteristics that show up in someone who had been sexually abused. Sandi's reaction was: *Why on earth would she give me this book?* When Sandi read it, she thought that this would be a good book to give to people who had been abused, and began to make lists of people who might be helped by it. But God spoke to Sandi gently. *Sandi, this is for you.* The book began to open up the memory. Sandi said:

It was almost like somebody dumped a jigsaw puzzle over—I recognized the individual pieces, but as they began to come together, I began to see a picture, and how abuse had affected my life.

Sometimes we try to anesthetize pain with sin, though the relief is short lived. We then discover greater pain and greater bondage.

Sandi's affair and divorce brought temporary relief and then greater pain, not only to herself, but to those close to her, and to the Lord Himself. Sandi also tried to hide her sin, but she was found out, for we can never hide from God, and He holds leaders, especially, to a high standard of accountability.

Sandi then confessed her sin openly to her church, later to *Christianity Today,* and to her public. She put herself under the authority of her church, and God used them to help her with the healing process. When I asked Sandi who had helped her during this time she said, quickly, "My church!"

What have they done? I asked.

They have really modeled for me what standing by and supporting someone means, she said.

And what does that mean?

It doesn't mean you agree with everything that person has done or support all the decisions that person has made. But you do not withdraw your love from them. It may mean difficult conversations, but it is not a lack of relationship.

You have sensed their love?

Oh yes! Sandi said. *They've been here for me. They really gave me a place to heal, a place for me to feel loved and safe so that I could be able to confront myself.*

On the other side, I commented, *you stayed with them. You didn't withdraw.*

Yes, I did. There were times when I didn't necessarily want to hear what they had to say, but I guess there was enough heritage in me that I knew that if I shut this door, if I let go of this life preserver, then I would really be lost, instead of just floundering.

When Sandi came to her first Heritage Keepers conference she began by confessing her sin. She also told about her discovery of being sexually abused as a child. Then she said:

*I don't make excuses for the choices I have made in my life. I am responsible. I am the one who has sinned. I am the one who has done things wrong. And I am accountable to make those things right before God. I am not saying these things in any way to make excuses. But, we must understand our past in order to put it behind and press on to what is ahead. We cannot stay stuck there. To make **excuses** means we are choosing to stay stuck, but to understand them as **reasons**, we are choosing to walk in truth, whatever that truth may be. Wherever there is truth, God is there, because He is truth. Even if that truth is ugly and horrible, if it is truth, He is there in the midst. It helps us to understand our past so we won't make the same mistakes again.*

Miriam, as you will soon see, also fell as an adult. No one is condoning the sins of either Miriam or Sandi, but when we consider the pain from their past, it builds compassion in us. Each of them, in the midst of their abuse, cried out to God, and He heard their groaning and had compassion on them, but that compassion did not lead to *instant* deliverance. For reasons known only to God, sometimes He allows His children to suffer the ravages of a sin sick world for a season.

So many women have experienced abuse in childhood. Perhaps you are one of them. At one Heritage Keepers conference, counselor Randy Storms talked about how Jesus had experienced abuse. So many women wrote and called to say what a comfort his words were that I share them, in part, here:

When we say, "Jesus, do you know what it is to be lonely?" Jesus says, *I know. The night I was betrayed I asked my closest friends to stand watch and to pray for me—and they couldn't do it.*

"But Jesus, do you know what it's like to be abused?"
Jesus says, *"I know. I've been whipped, they drove nails into my hands, I hung on the cross."*

"But Jesus, do you know what it's like to be sexually abused?"
Jesus says, *They stripped me of my clothes and I hung on that cross with shame as people walked by. I know what it's like.*

When we say to Jesus, "It hurts to be human." He says, *I know. I've been there. I've been there. And I want to come and comfort you.*

Despite the pain that both Miriam and Sandi experienced in childhood, though they were the walking wounded, still, God used them each mightily as adult women.

MIRIAM, A PROPHETESS, A LEADER, A WOMAN GIFTED IN SONG

For many, the knowledge of Miriam stops with her as the big sister who protectively stood guard over her brother's basket in the Nile. But Miriam grew up to become the first female prophet and a leader of women. Miriam watched God perform miracle after miracle, through Moses, to convince the Pharaoh to let the Hebrew people go. (Psalm 78:44-53 describes some of the miracles Miriam witnessed.)

After God opened the Red Sea for the Israelites and closed it over the pursuing Egyptian armies, we are told:

Then Miriam the prophetess, Aaron's sister, took a tambourine in her hand, and all the women followed her, with tambourines and dancing. Miriam sang to them:

"Sing to the Lord, for he is highly exalted.
The horse and its rider he has hurled into the sea." (Exodus 15:20)

And though that song was sung thousands of years ago, it is still being sung. One of our family's favorite praise songs is "The Horse and Rider":

I will sing unto the Lord, for He has triumphed gloriously
the horse and rider fell into the sea ...

Miriam and her music is having an impact. She impacted her generation, the next generation, and generations tumbling out in millenniums to come.

SANDI, A LEADER, A WOMAN GIFTED IN SONG

I remember the first time our family saw Sandi in concert. She absolutely thrilled the audience. Her voice, her range, and the emotion with which she sang lifted us into the presence of God. We drove home from Omaha singing along with one of her tapes:

> *Oh magnify, oh magnify, the Lord with me and let us exalt His name together....*

Our children bought her album *Sandi Patty & The Friendship Company* and played it constantly. Her Christmas album was my all-time favorite. The featured song, "The Gift Goes On," always reminds me of the Heritage Keepers' theme: *From generation to generation.* Sandi and her music is having an impact: on her generation, the next generation, and the children yet to be born.

MIRIAM'S FALL

I found the cartoon version of Exodus, *Prince of Egypt,* exceedingly well done and, for the most part, scripturally accurate. Many cautioned parents not to take very young children to it, saying children would be frightened or bored. However, if children have been told the story of Moses, if they have grasped the wonder through the teaching of their parents, I think they will be blessed by it. Our granddaughters, Emily (five) and Jessamyn (three), loved *Prince of Egypt.* I asked them what they liked best about the movie. Emily's eyes grew round, her arms raised dramatically, and she took a deep breath: "Oh Grammy, didn't you love it when God parted the sea?" And Jessamyn laughed and bobbed her head up and down, agreeing: "Da water and da fishes!"

I smiled at their wonder, and thanked God for it. Yet seeing it on a cartoon certainly pales to *being there.* Miriam was one who witnessed it all. Beginning from the time she was a little girl, she saw God *move* on behalf of His people, again, and again, and again. She felt, firsthand, the fear of being chased by the Egyptian chariots and being trapped by the Red Sea. She saw the waters divide, the enormous walls rise and stand, being held back by the invisible hands of God. *She* and the other Israelites walked through, trusting in God as they did. Certainly you would expect Miriam, Aaron, and all of the Israelites who had witnessed the extraordinary deliverance of God to live exemplary lives, continually putting their hope in such a mighty God. But Psalm 78 makes it clear they did not.

> *They forgot what he had done, the wonders he had shown them....*
> *How often they rebelled against him in the desert*
> *and grieved him in the wasteland!* (Psalm 78:11, 40)

Miriam was one who grieved God in the wasteland. The account of her personal sin is in Numbers 12.

Moses had taken a new wife, perhaps after the death of Zipporah, and she was a Cushite, and therefore, probably black. Miriam, weary of playing second fiddle to Moses, decided to pick on his new wife. (How like human nature! When we are jealous, we look for the soft underside, the vulnerable portion. Instead of attacking Moses, Miriam attacked his wife. I picture her criticizing her sister-in-law's cooking, figure, and, maybe, her skin color.) Finally Miriam began grumbling about what was *really* troubling her, enlisting the sympathy of brother Aaron.

> *Has the Lord spoken only through Moses? Hasn't he also spoken through us?* (Numbers 12:2a)

And then, in a chilling phrase, we are told:

> *And the Lord heard this.* (Exodus 12:2b)

Of course the Lord hears everything. There is no such thing as a secret sin. We cannot hide from His presence. But sometimes He restrains His anger. Psalm 78:38-39 tells us:

> *Time after time he restrained his anger*
> *and did not stir up his full wrath.*
> *He remembered that they were but flesh,*
> *a passing breeze that does not return.*

Other times, however, He calls us to account immediately. Often, He acts quickly with those in spiritual leadership. Imagine their fear when the following occurred:

At once the Lord said to Moses, Aaron and Miriam, "Come out to the Tent of Meeting, all three of you." So the three of them came out. Then the Lord came down in a pillar of cloud; he stood at the entrance to the Tent and summoned Aaron and Miriam. When both of them stepped forward, he said, "Listen to my words:

"When a prophet of the Lord is among you,
I reveal myself to him in visions, I speak to him in dreams.
But this is not true of my servant Moses;
he is faithful in all my house. With him I speak face to face,
clearly and not in riddles; he sees the form of the Lord.
Why then were you not afraid to speak against my servant Moses?"

The anger of the Lord burned against them, and he left them. When the cloud lifted from above the Tent, there stood Miriam—leprous, like snow. Aaron turned toward her and saw that she had leprosy; and he said to Moses, "Please, my lord, do not hold against us the sin we have so foolishly committed. Do not let her be like a stillborn infant coming from its mother's womb with its flesh half eaten away." (Numbers 12:4-12)

Why did God discipline Miriam—and not Aaron? In Numbers 12:1 Miriam's name is listed first, and the Hebrew uses a feminine verb for "spoke," leading us to believe she, and not Aaron, was the instigator. Why does He make her white with leprosy? If she *had* made negative comments about the skin color of the new wife it would be a fitting discipline. However, it is clear the primary sin was jealousy and it angered God. He expected much more of Miriam, who had been blessed, delivered, and loved. Though He knew she had suffered as a child, He still held her accountable for her choices. God is both a God of mercy and a God of justice.

Moses, though he was the one who was sinned against, intercedes for his sister, whom he obviously loves:

Moses cried out to the Lord, "O God, please heal her!" (Numbers 12:13)

And God did. He forgave Miriam and healed her. Yet her sin had consequences. In fact, it affected the whole body of believers, as sin always does. When Miriam sinned she was confined for seven days outside the camp. For seven days thousands of people were inconvenienced. Can't you just imagine the questions, the whisperings? *Why can't we break camp? What is the problem?* Jesus compares sin to yeast: it begins as a little lump but spreads, affecting the whole loaf. Confining Miriam was a lesson, not just for her, but for the whole body. It was similar to the lesson God gave the Israelites when He told them to get rid of all the yeast in their homes before Passover. God was saying: *Get rid of sin. I hate it! It hurts everyone.* No matter how quietly we sin, that sin spreads. Like a pebble tossed in a pond, the ripples affect not only those near and dear, but those further out, even generations to come.

GOD EXPECTS MORE OF HIS CHOSEN PEOPLE

Os Guiness, in *The Call*, says that being chosen by God brings a heavier burden, and a sterner judgment.[6] And for those who have been given the privilege of public ministry, the judgment is sterner still. Surely there were other sisters-in-law among the Israelites who envied, who grumbled, and who were not struck with leprosy. But if you are a leader, God will often rebuke you in public because He is concerned about the body. We can all think of wonderful Christian singers, evangelists, and pastors who have sinned privately and been caught. Have you ever wondered why God airs all of our dirty laundry before the world, why a Christian leader cannot seem to sin and get away with it? It is because God is concerned about His heritage. James warns us:

> Not many of you should presume to be teachers, my brothers, because you know that we who teach will be judged more strictly. (James 3:1)

How does God want a leader to respond when He rebukes him or her? He wants no excuses, but complete repentance. If you study leaders in the Scripture who fell, some were restored, and some were not—the difference seems to lie in how they responded to God's rebuke.

THE LORD IS CLOSE TO THE BROKENHEARTED

I believe Sandi's response *has* been pleasing to God, which is perhaps why He also seems to be restoring her ministry. ABC television had Sandi Patty and Amy Grant on *PrimeTime Live* shortly before Heritage Keepers reached out to Sandi.[7] The hosts seemed particularly eager to air dirty laundry, for the world is eager to discredit Christianity. I found their comments and reactions sad, revealing tremendous spiritual blindness and confusion, for though they were eager to point out Sandi's failings, they simultaneously seemed surprised that Sandi was taking it so very seriously. Yet despite the blindness from the writers and hosts of *PrimeTime*, Sandi's response shows a woman longing to be right with God, a woman who is accepting God's discipline. The interviewer couldn't really understand Sandi's heart. Even Diane Sawyer's opening seemed to imply that this fall will hurt her sales, which they saw as the main issue. Here are some excerpts from *PrimeTime Live*.

Diane Sawyer: *To make it big in Christian rock, a singer's image can be as important as the music....*

Jay Schadler: *Sandi Patty may be Christian music's greatest vocalist. But this woman who sings like an angel has had a devil of a time in her private life, and now her public will judge her secrets and sins.*

Sandi Patty: *And if that means losing my career, then so be it. If that means having people find out the junk in my life, then so be it. But I cannot carry the weight of my sin....*

Jay: *You broke one of the Ten Commandments?*

Sandi: *Absolutely. I mean, that's huge. That's nothing to gloss over. I recognize that. That is huge.*

Jay: *... If affairs and divorce sometimes seem the norm on the pop scene, in Sandi's world, they are eternal sins.*

Sandi: *There are consequences that will never go away. You know, that's always part of my story. Always, forever and ever.*

Jay: *In fact, after filing for divorce, Sandi's own church released this statement, saying Sandi "carries a sense of shame and a scarlet letter that will haunt her as long as she lives."*

Sandi: *I'm very supportive of that from the standpoint that…*

Jay: (interrupts with surprise) *You carry a scarlet letter? You're supportive of that?*

Sandi: *I think what they're saying is, we can clearly see she recognizes the damage—lifelong damage that has been done.*

Sandi, in commenting on the above interview, said to me, "Out of an incredibly wonderful three-page letter from my church, *PrimeTime* pulled the comment about the scarlet letter, truly, I think, out of context. My *church* wasn't putting a scarlet letter on me, they were simply saying, "We know Sandi, she'll always carry this sense of shame. She doesn't take this lightly."

After her fall and confession, Sandi received lots of mail. She wrote everybody back, including the angry fans. She said, "I understand. I know I let you down. I let God down. I let myself down. I understand your anger and it's okay. Thank you for taking the time to be honest, owning your feelings, and letting me know."

"Wow," I said, thinking of how beautifully Sandi modeled how to respond to ungrace.

"And you know, Dee, every single person who wrote an angry letter wrote me back and said, 'I could have said it a lot differently and in a more loving way. I guess I don't understand, but I am praying for you.' That was pretty awesome."

Sandi knows that even if more and more people give her grace, there will always be consequences. There will always be pain.

Perhaps that is why, when referring to Miriam, the Bible says:

Remember what the Lord your God did to Miriam along the way after you came out of Egypt. (Deuteronomy 24:9)

Why does God tell us to remember? So that we
Miriam? No. So that we can realize that sin is seriou
wander into the darkness, we may also experience the
God. I'm sure there were those in the camp who had troub
Miriam, who grumbled against her, and who felt cold when sh
lead them in praise songs. They *forgot* about how God had shown
grace, had led them out of slavery, and had delivered them from t
enemies. So they couldn't show grace to Miriam. However, our God is:

AGAINST FORGETTING OUR HOLY HERITAGE

And there were a few (though very few, I suspect, in that rebellious generation), who gave Miriam grace. They thought about the hard times she had experienced as a child, they thought about their own sinful nature, the sinful choices they had made and wished they could undo, they thought about how much grace God had shown them—and they gave her grace. They did not condone her sin, and in fact, it put the fear of God in them and they took it as a lesson to avoid sinning, but they embraced her, loved her, and received her back into the family of God.

WHO WILL THROW THE FIRST STONE?

How are we going to respond to Sandi? I think we need to respond to her as Jesus does. He does not condone her sin. He grieves over the heartache she has brought to her family and the family of God. Sandi's church in Anderson, Indiana has sought God's face in how to deal with their erring child. Because she is repentant, because she has submitted herself to their guidance, which includes being accountable to a panel of godly people, they are giving her grace. The question they asked themselves was *What would Jesus do?* Jim Lyon, the senior pastor at Sandi's church, North Anderson Church of God, wrote me, saying:

> *Sandi made two important choices as she came to terms with her own sin: (1) she owned the truth about herself, and (2) she resisted the temptation to run away (from her church, her community, her relationships, her Lord). These choices have made it possible for us to work with her, for Heaven's sake and her good.*

tely:

...tone? Sandi has confessed and paid
...lo so. She is submitting herself to the
...st go on.

...pick up their tents and move on
...ation, so must we. Sandi is our
...e do not show her compassion,
...ld the character of compassion

After Sandi's first appearance at Heritage Keepers, Lori came up on the stage and put her arm around her and turned to the audience. She thanked Sandi and then, gently, said,

Who of us here has not failed? Who has not sinned?

Lori reminded me, at the moment, of Barnabas, the man who helped the body of Christ receive Saul, who had persecuted Christians, even to their deaths. Barnabas took Saul and brought him to the apostles, telling them of how Saul had seen the Lord, how the Lord had spoken to him, and how Barnabas had seen the fruit of repentance in Saul.

When we cannot forgive, we become the one who grieves God, for we have been forgiven so much. Repetition is a clue, in Scripture, as to what is important to God, and there are so many verses about the importance of forgiving others that there is not room to list them, but here are a few:

Be kind and compassionate to one another, forgiving each other, just as in Christ God forgave you. (Ephesians 4:32)

Do not judge, and you will not be judged. Do not condemn, and you will not be condemned. Forgive, and you will be forgiven. (Luke 6:37)

Then Peter came to Jesus and asked, "Lord, how many times shall I forgive my brother when he sins against me? Up to seven times?" Jesus answered,

"I tell you, not seven times, but seventy-seven times." (Matthew 18:21)

Following the above answer to Peter, Jesus tells the parable of the unmerciful servant. It is a convicting parable that ends with the master turning the unmerciful servant over to the jailers to be tortured! If this doesn't put the fear of God into us, I don't know what will.

THE POWER OF GRACE AND THE POWER OF UNGRACE

I think one of the reasons the Becklers were able to extend grace to Sandi is because they had experienced its healing power themselves. Lori explains:

My family in Wichita was practically Pollyanna Utopia, but Bob's family experienced one tragedy after another. When Bob was fourteen, his little brother Michael, who was just seven, developed lymphoma. An inoperable tumor tightened around Michael's esophagus and he went into a coma. For ten days the family paced in the hospital while the doctors told them he was already gone—except for the machines. Finally they made the very hard decision to turn off the life support system. And, as the statistics sadly show, the death of a child is often followed by the death of a marriage. So it was with Bob's parents.

Shortly after Bob and Lori married, Bob's parents divorced. Lori's eyes filled with tears, for the pain of wrong choices never completely fades. "What happened," I asked, "to Bob's relationship with his dad?"

Lori stood up and walked to the window, looking out at the sky. She turned to me and said:

Bob fought for a relationship with his dad. He showed him grace. But still, those were painful years. I think any child of divorce, no matter how old, still yearns to see his mother and father together. But that never happened with Bob's parents—not even for holidays—there was just too much pain. And then, Bob's mother married Joe Yount, a fine Christian widower whom we love. Bob's dad has remained single.

"And what is the relationship like now between Bob's mother and father?" I asked.

Reflectively, Lori said:

One of the great blessings of this ministry of Heritage Keepers is how it has brought us together as a family. Bob's mother and her new husband began to help with Heritage Keepers—and then Bob's dad, I think because Bob had maintained a relationship with him, began to help as well. As we all worked, as a family, putting on the conferences, the walls began to come down. Gradually Bob's mom and dad began to be more comfortable being together. It was as if a little hole had been drilled in the dam that had been holding back grace, and now it began to trickle through.

Then, after a few Heritage Keepers conferences, Bob and his brother Rick had an idea. Lori explained:

Bob had not spent Christmas with both of his parents since 1981, but in 1997, Bob suggested the whole family, including his mother, her new husband, his dad, grandparents, and siblings spend Christmas together. He'd been encouraged by the grace he'd seen at the conferences, so he thought perhaps they were ready to all be together.

"And what happened?" I asked.

God is so good. Bob's dad was so glad to be invited. He flew out from California with gifts for everyone—even for Bob's mother and her new husband. Grampa started telling stories about the Titanic and pretty soon we were into family stories—the good things we could remember. We played cards and, at Christmas dinner, Bob's dad and stepdad sat next to each other. We talked about Heritage Keepers—and several shared they were thankful God was using this ministry to bring healing in the family. It was a tender time—a time when we saw that hole widen in the dam and grace began to truly flow. There will always be scars and sadness about the losses, but life can still have meaning and hope.

The Becklers could have held onto their hurts and passed ungrace to the next generation. Instead, they chose to give grace and it involved each and every family member, for each had experienced genuine hurts. (Sin is never isolated; it always spreads, like gangrene, hurting the whole body.) Undoubtedly, you, too, as a member of the human race, have experienced hurts from choices that members in your family have made. I have appreciated Philip Yancey's emphasis in *What's So Amazing About Grace*. He says that it is *costly* to give grace. When someone has hurt you, it is unnatural to forgive them. What is natural is to want them to suffer—at least a little! Grace, though absolutely free to the recipient, can be very costly to the giver. There is only one thing that is more costly than giving grace, Yancey says, and that is the alternative. For either grace is passed on from generation to generation, or ungrace is passed down. Families, tribes, and nations are destroyed through ungrace.[8]

I don't think it is coincidental that the family founding Heritage Keepers would be tested in this area of grace. I am convinced that God is as concerned that we learn how to pass on grace as He is concerned that we pass on the stories that reflect His grace. The Becklers passed the test, and we are all richer because of it.

I also find it intriguing, that shortly after the Becklers had experienced the healing power of grace, that a decision needed to be made concerning whether or not to give grace to Sandi Patty and extend an invitation to her to minister at Heritage Keepers.

REACHING OUT TO SANDI

Sandi's name had been suggested frequently as a possibility for Heritage Keepers. Lori said,

> I'll be honest. Though I absolutely loved her music, because of the controversy, I simply didn't want to go there. But her name kept coming up, and we found out Point of Grace wasn't going to be able to be with us at our third engagement in Wichita in June of 1998. So, I thought I'd be willing to talk to Sandi and hear her heart, but frankly, I wasn't particularly open.

Then, during the next two weeks, Lori's devotions centered on grace and God's forgiveness. The day before Lori was to talk to Sandi, Lori opened her *Women's Devotional Bible*, which she hardly ever uses, and read a devotional about how we as Christians do not take care of our wounded. We condemn. *How,* the devotional asked, *can there ever be healing if we as Christians don't show God's grace to a brother or a sister who has fallen?* So Lori contacted Sandi's manager.

When Sandi heard that Lori had called, she drilled her manager: "Are you sure they want me? Do they know everything? Are you positive?"

Her manager said, "Yes. We had a wonderful talk. Lori is aware of everything in your past, and she knows what you've gone through with your church in the healing process. She wants to talk to you on the phone."

Sandi couldn't believe God was opening this door—and she was nervous about the phone call, almost to the point of tears. She said, "The first thing Lori said was: 'Sandi, I just know God loves you and we love you.' She totally put my spirit at ease and really gave me the gift of grace, extending her love. Her voice was so full of love and acceptance—no shame at all."

Lori remembers:

I could see Sandi's heart—it was broken, repentant. We prayed together, asking God to show us His will. Soon I knew that if I did not invite her that I would be being disobedient. How could I, who had been shown so much grace, refuse to offer grace to my repentant sister?

"And what," I asked, "has been the response to Sandi?"

People who had condemned her—or us, for inviting her—wrote letters of apology. Others wrote and said that they were thankful to see that God is a God of grace. The forgiveness and restoration of Sandi gave them hope that God could forgive and restore them.

GRACE NOTES

The need to give grace applies not only to major transgressions, but to the minor transgressions that occur all day long: the spilled milk, the lost library book, and the dirty socks on the floor. Either a melody of grace sounds throughout our homes or the heavy organ chords of judgment, and often, the mother sets the tone. Solomon says:

The wise woman builds her house, but with her own hands the foolish one tears hers down. (Proverbs 14:1)

How do we build up our house, our children? With grace notes! Here are a few of the ways my parents handed grace to me:

My earliest memories are of my mother lifting me from my crib, singing, always singing, and holding me close to her cheek, which always smelled of Pond's Cold Cream.

When I was nine my dad bought me a camera and suggested I write a book, with pictures, about my dog. When I did he praised me to the heavens and made twenty-five copies of My Dog Chloe *to give to friends and relatives. (They in turn gave me grace by sending me dear notes to build me up, and not one mentioned my spelling errors or my unusual logic, for I had put Chloe's muddy pawprint on each cover and had written: "This book is all true. The paw print proves it.")*

Mother gave me the freedom to put a blond streak in my hair when I was thirteen. (I looked like a skunk.)

When I failed them, and I have broken their hearts, they continued to love me. They believed in me and refused to judge me by my weakest moment.

Our home was filled with music, laughter, praise, and hugs: grace notes.

Part of showing our children love is training them to obey us and to speak respectfully to us and others when they are young. But we also have a responsibility to show grace, or we will make our children feel like giving up (Ephesians 6:4). Home needs to be a haven—not a place where you are going to be continually torn down because your hygiene, or your grammar, or your bedroom falls short of the glory of God.

I am blessed with a wonderful husband whose spiritual gift is mercy. I can count on one hand the number of times he has criticized me in thirty-five years of marriage. I love to be around him. Likewise, he is filled with mercy toward our children.

When we adopted Beth, who had spent the first twelve years of her life in an orphanage in Bangkok, I was aghast at her manners. She shoveled food into her mouth, burped, and spit. How did my husband respond? He smiled gently. He knew that to try to change everything in her at once would have destroyed her. I am absolutely convinced that his grace toward Beth is the reason we are seeing some success in what is statistically a high-risk adoption. She feels loved and accepted by him, and she wants to please him. My husband's example and the wise counsel of authors in the body of Christ is equipping me to give grace. (If you haven't read John Trent and Gary Smalley's *The Blessing*, do! It is filled with ways to give grace notes.) My knee-jerk response to Beth was to want to flood her with rules, to pummel her into shape. However, my husband has helped me to see the power of grace. Mike Yorkey, author of *Faithful Parents, Faithful Kids* wrote:

> *Behavior was important, but relationship was the bullseye.*[9]

When our children feel loved and valued, often the rest falls into place. If we want to keep our kids close, if we want to see the melody of grace flowing to the next generation, we'd better fill our home with grace notes.

AND THE GIFT GOES ON

When we give to others the grace God has given us, then they are restored and replenished and able to give grace to the next generation. One of the most incredible stories that Sandi tells is how God led her and Don to adopt a baby.

She and Don had seven children between them, but sometimes

they would talk about how fun it would be to add a child between them. Don was adopted and said he would love to, therefore, adopt. And if they had a boy, they dreamed, they would name him Sam, after Don's father. Sandi laughed, "But then we would slap each other back to reality and say, 'Forget it!'"

One day Sandi flippantly said to God, "If You want us to adopt, would You just drop a baby in our lap?"

Several months later Sandi received a call from her dear friend Sherri, whose husband handles private adoptions. Sandi was very quiet when Sherri asked:

Sandi, do you know of anyone who is looking to adopt? We have a baby who was born two days ago and the adoption fell through at the last minute. We've called everybody on our list, and they called people, and they called people. The baby is going into welfare tomorrow if nobody takes this baby. Do you know of anyone who is looking to adopt?

Sandi said, "I can't believe you are calling me with this." *Was God on the move?* Sandi and Don called their pastor. Then they had a family meeting. The kids said, as only kids could, "Let's go and get the baby!"

Sandi said, "It's not that simple."

Sandi's mind was racing. *This doesn't make sense intellectually—but God, are You leading? What do we do?* They decided that if another family turned up before the next day that they would trust that was God's plan—otherwise, they would throw out a fleece. (Or, as Sandi's son calls it, "a blanket.")

No other family turned up. The next day Sandi said, "I felt compelled—something just literally pushing me to go see this baby. I didn't even know if that was permissible, so I called Sherri. She made some calls, worked it out, and we were in the car on the way to see the baby.

Sherri and her husband met Sandi and Don at the hospital. Sherri said, "You guys, we've got to pray." Sandi asked God for "a smack-you-in-the-face burning bush"—a sign to help them know for sure, one way or another.

God gave them exactly that, for when Sherri wheeled the bassinet back to Sandi and Don, she was crying. Immediately Sandi thought something was wrong. But then she too saw the little name tag at the end of the crib:

Sandi and Don looked at each other. They knew that often people don't name babies who are to be put up for adoption. Sandi and Don burst into tears. "His name is Sam!" they cried.

The nurse in the room was confused. She said, "You don't have to keep that name."

Sandi and Don brought Sam home that very day and they have definitely seen God's hand in this plan. Sandi told me how Sam has been a catalyst in helping their family to become one:

A blended family is very tough. It has some wonderful things and it has some very challenging things, especially for the kids, for this was not their choice, and there is a lot of territorial stuff that goes on. But when Sam came into our home, nobody could define him as mine or yours. He was definitely ours. I think even if I had birthed Sam, it wouldn't have had the same positive impact as adopting. He is truly a gift to all of us.

I couldn't stop my own tears as Sandi continued:

When I saw the rainbows around Sam's name, it was very significant to me. When God gave a rainbow for the first time, it was to promise there would never be a storm like that again. Don and I had walked through some tremendous storms, which were nobody's fault but our own, but now I felt that God was saying, "I promise you new life—not just figuratively, but literally, with Sam." For God to entrust us with this life, Samuel, meaning God has heard, has been such a wonderful reminder of God's active love in our lives.

After Sandi told this incredible story at Heritage Keepers she sang "Somewhere over the Rainbow," as only Sandi can. I thought, *God is restoring Sandi.* Because of her truly repentant heart, many are able to hear her music again and to be ministered to by her music again. I have also been challenged by Sandi's vulnerability as I have worked with her on this chapter—and it has made me want to be honest and vulnerable so that I too can go to a deeper level with God.

When Sam was three, he came on stage with Sandi at Heritage Keepers. She held him, an adorable little boy with wild brown curls, saucer eyes, and just a touch of mocha in his skin. Sandi said, "Sam is one-third African-American, one-third American Indian, and one-third Caucasian. Sam for president!" He smiled at her broadly, and when she told the story about how he'd come to a big white house, with lots and lots of kids, and lots and lots of love, he finished her sentences, for he knew the story well. She was helping him remember how God had worked in his life, so that he would one day tell his children. Then Sandi sang to Sam, and he laid his head on her shoulder, smiling. As Sam's precious face was caught by the cameraman and magnified on the five screens around the arena, we could see the power of transforming love.

And the gift goes on.

Panning for Heritage Gold

☼ Icebreaker: Throw out the following words or phrases to the group and ask them to toss back associations they bring to mind:

a gracious woman

gratis

ingrate

persona non grata

What did the above exercise teach you about grace or ungrace?

1. Explain what stood out to you from the text and Scriptures in chapter 10. Why?

Read the following passages as an overview and highlight anything you learn about Miriam: Exodus 2:1-10; Exodus 15:19-21; Numbers 12; and Deuteronomy 24:9.

☼ 2. What do you learn about Miriam's parents in Hebrews 11:23?

3. Read Exodus 2:1-10 and, using your imagination, how do you think Jochebed might have mentored her daughter Miriam during this time?

4. How does Jochebed fit the qualifications for being "a daughter of Sarah?"

5. How do you see God at work in this story? Give references.

6. What was good about the childhood of Miriam? What was difficult?

7. Describe some of the miracles Miriam witnessed as the adult sister of Moses. (See Exodus 4-15 and/or Psalm 78:12-16).

8. What are some of the blessings of your personal heritage? If you had godly parents or mentors, how did they bless you?

9. What were some of the hardships from your childhood that could make you vulnerable to wrong choices? (For example, the child of an alcoholic is more apt to abuse alcohol and the child of divorced parents is more apt to divorce.)

Based on the above awareness, what precautions might you take to help you avoid wrong choices?

Read Exodus 15:19-21.

10. Describe how God used Miriam as an adult.

Read Numbers 12.

11. With verse references, describe:

    A. Miriam's attitude and sin

B. God's rebuke to Miriam

C. Moses' response

D. God's response to Moses

12. Why do you think God gives the command He does in Deuteronomy 24:9?

13. What did you learn from the parallel made between Sandi Patty and Miriam?

14. God restores some fallen leaders, and others never seem to be in a leadership position again. What makes the difference? David is one whom God restored after his great sin. (2 Samuel 11) What do you see in David's life in the following passages?:

A. 2 Samuel 12:13

B. Psalm 51

15. Is there anything blocking fellowship between you and God? Confess and turn from your sin.

☀ 16. Meditate on Matthew 18:21-35

A. How does Jesus answer Peter's question? (vv. 21-22) What do you think this means?

B. Describe what happens in the story Jesus tells.

C. What point is Jesus making?

D. There is forgiveness that "appears" to be forgiveness, but is not. Describe that kind of forgiveness. Then contrast it with the forgiveness Jesus describes in verse 35. Describe that.

17. Philip Yancey says that it is hard to give grace, because it is costly. What can giving grace cost you?

However, Yancey says, *not* giving grace is costlier. What can not giving grace do to:

    A. your family?

    B. the next generation?

    C. your fellowship with God?

18. What is God impressing on your heart from this lesson?

PRAYER TIME:

Have each woman lift up her own request and allow the others to support her with sentence prayers.

Eleven

> *Let us see ourselves in the Lord's ancient people, and bemoan*
> *our own provocations of the Most High, at the same time*
> *admiring his infinite patience, and adoring him because of it.*[1]
>
> CHARLES SPURGEON

Against Forgetting

*W*isconsin, that mitten-shaped state, has a gorgeous thumb called Door County, a densely wooded peninsula that juts into Lake Michigan. My husband and I are alone here together at our cabin this week, where God has been restoring our minds and our spirits through His Creation and His Word. On a stormy, day as Steve sat by the fire in an overstuffed chair, he gazed out at the wild surf, just fifteen feet away. As waves crested into whitecaps and crashed upon the shore, Steve thought: *The water is so powerful—we are at its mercy. Who can control the sea?* With this question as the last thought in his conscious mind, he then fell asleep.

Upon awakening, Steve reached for his leather Bible, flipped it open at the bookmark, and began reading Psalm 114. Here was yet another account of Israel's departure from Egypt:

> *The sea looked and fled, the Jordan turned back;*
> *the mountains skipped like rams, the hills like lambs.*
> *Why was it, O sea, that you fled, O Jordan, that you turned back,*
> *you mountains, that you skipped like rams, you hills, like lambs?*
> *Tremble, O earth, at the presence of the Lord, at the presence*
> *of the God of Jacob....* (vv.3-7)

Steve said, in awe, "I felt like God was talking to me, reminding me that He controls the sea."

God wants us to be:

Against forgetting our holy heritage

Charles Spurgeon says, "Shame upon us that we should let slip what it would seem impossible to forget."[2] If we would keep these things in our remembrance, we would walk by faith, and not by sight. For just as He opened the Red Sea for the Israelites, just as He rolled back the Jordan, He can surmount "problems" as seemingly overwhelming as becoming the parents of septuplets or of paying for the rental of Market Square Arena in Indianapolis.

Just as He called to Abraham, to Moses, and to Miriam, He calls to us. He still speaks, sometimes through His Spirit, as He did with Lori Beckler, Sandi Patty, and me—but most frequently He speaks through His Word.

He has recorded the incidents of our holy heritage not just for Noah's ark nursery wallpaper or for Hollywood blockbusters, but so that we may learn about our holy God. He wants us to remember His power, He wants us to learn from our ancestors, and to see ourselves in their lives. To do that we must get below the surface and understand the message of each story, and also, how they fit together.

In this chapter we'll look again at some of those golden nuggets. Reviewing is key to be:

Against forgetting our holy heritage

This can be a powerful time in your devotional or small group time to help you store those golden nuggets in your memory bank rather than letting them slip to the bottom of the river.

EVE

If you remember, one of the first nuggets we panned was that there is a snake in the grass who targets women. He hopes we will take our husbands and children by the hands and lead them down the path toward destruction. It makes sense to slither toward the *relational sex*. Why aim for just one when you can have a whole family?

In the very beginning Satan targeted Eve, and she led her husband astray. Generations later, Satan targeted Sarah, and she led her husband astray. Millenniums later Satan targeted Lori, trying to keep her from founding Heritage Keepers. We have an ancient foe.

Satan will try to lure us off the path with temptations, feeding us the lie that the temptation will actually be good for us. Unless we are immersed in God's Word, we will be likely to fall for his line. A common ploy is to make mothers busy, too busy to pass on the heritage.

Remember how he lured Lori with the temptation of wealth and power? She nearly forgot about God's call for a woman's conference. And when Heritage Keepers was blessed with numerical success, Christian publishers were eager to jump on the bandwagon and say: Promote our product and schedule thirty Heritage Keepers events a year! I have so respected the restraint of Lori and Bob. Lori said, "In four years we will be empty nesters, and then we may increase the number of Heritage Keepers conferences. But right now, our top priority is Nicole and Daniel." So, for now, Heritage Keepers is limiting their events.

Dr. James Dobson often tells of the pressure on him to go on tour when his children were little. But he stood firm.

How like the Enemy to try to divert the founder of Focus on the Family from his own family, or the founders of Heritage Keepers from keeping the heritage!

Likewise, the Enemy tries to divert us from leading a quiet life (1 Timothy 2:2). If we are constantly driving our children to gymnastics, Girl Scouts, the video store, or even church activities, we are distracted from the quiet home life that enables us to pass on the heritage.

Last fall a young mother named Kim, who was pregnant with her fourth son, confessed, as she sat in my living room: "We've taught our sons how to play soccer. We've provided them with music lessons. We've helped them with their geometry. But I've been asking myself: have we given them the most precious inheritance of all? Have we really impressed on their hearts the truths of God?"

Home schooling brings families back to the quiet life, where, instead of being whirled about like straws upon a river, they live reflective lives, choosing what is most important. There is time to love, to talk, and to pass down the heritage. But even if God has not led you to home school, you can still choose the quiet life. You can keep out the twenty hours of television watching or the myriad of activities that are clogging the flow of the pure river of God.

Catherine Marshall, whom you may know as the author of *Christy*, also wrote, before most of you were born, a biography of her famous husband, *A Man Called Peter*. Peter Marshall, a handsome Scot with a deep voice and rolling *r's*, was one of the most beloved preachers of all time. In a famous Mother's Day sermon titled *Keepers of the Springs*, he told a story:

> *Once upon a time, a certain town grew up at the foot of a mountain range.... High in the hills, a strange and quiet forest dweller took it upon himself to be the Keeper of the Springs.*

> *He patrolled the hills and wherever he found a spring, he cleaned its brown pool of silt and fallen leaves, of mud and mould and took away from the spring all foreign matter, so that the water which bubbled up through the sand ran down clean and cold and pure.*

> *It leaped sparkling over rocks and dropped joyously in crystal cascades until, swollen by other streams, it became a river of life to the busy town.*

But the city council decided the Keeper of the Springs was an unnecessary expense, and fired him. Soon the delicate machinery of the mills was clogged with slime, the swans found another home, and an epidemic raged, and the clammy, yellow fingers of sickness reached into every home in every street and lane.

Then this Scottish preacher cried out:

Do not think me fanciful
too imaginative
or too extravagant in my language

When I say that I think of women
and particularly of our mothers,
as Keepers of the Springs.[3]

As mothers, we are the primary caretakers in our children's lives in their formative years. This is part of God's call on our lives, for when God came to Adam and Eve He told them that the Fall would affect each of them in different ways: with Eve, it was in regard to being a mother; with Adam, it was in regard to his work. That is not to say that fathers are not called to parent, for clearly they are, but that the nurturing power of a mother can make an enormous difference in the spiritual, emotional, and physical health of a child. She is *the keeper of the spring.* How like Satan to want her to ignore her calling so that "the clammy, yellow fingers of sickness will reach every street and lane." Remember, Satan targets you as a woman, because you have enormous influence. You must stay in the Word. You must stay on the path.

One of the most emotional experiences of my life was flying to Bangkok, Thailand, where we went to the orphanage to pick up our new daughter, Beth. The adoption agency had chosen twelve of the five hundred children from that orphanage whom they called *survivors.* These were the children who they thought might make it as adoptees. What had these children survived? Being deprived of the nurturing love of a mother. Most of the children in that orphanage rocked back and forth and stared at us with blank, expressionless eyes. Are mothers important? Satan knows they are.

Many mothers have abandoned their calling, feeling unvalued by the world. But God values you, as a mother or a mentor, and He has called you to be a keeper of the springs.

Let me ask you to consider some questions: *Where is your focus? Are you, like Martha, distracted and worried about many things? Does your family live a quiet life? Are you so abiding in Christ that you can spot the lies of the Enemy? Are you so abiding in Christ that the pure love of God springs from you and splashes on those around you?*

SARAH

Instead of being daughters of Eve, God longs for us to be daughters of Sarah.

In part, that means working as a team. If you are married, it means respecting your husband and believing God can speak through him. Likewise, he should do the same with you. Adam and Eve failed to check each other, but, generally speaking, Abraham and Sarah were a good team, each seeking God and sharing with one another. The only times they got into trouble were when they forgot to do this.

Being a daughter of Sarah also means living by faith, and not giving way, as 1 Peter 3:6 says, "to hysterical fears." It is easy to trust God when things are going well; it is quite another when the road becomes rough.

When Peter told women to be like Sarah it was in the context of extreme persecution. Christians were being burned as human torches. Believing wives were being severely persecuted by their unbelieving husbands. Peter advises them to look to their holy heritage, to Sarah, and to do as she did.

What did she do? She trusted God, clinging to Him as she sojourned on earth. She was a respectful and supportive wife to her spiritual giant of a husband. When he felt led to do things that would have frightened most of us, she set her hope in God and did not give way to hysterical fears.

Let me ask you: *Are you working as a team with your husband, or, if you are single, with others in the body of Christ? Do you individually seek God's face and seek to be like-minded in Him? What causes you fear and anxiety right now? Will you be a true daughter of Sarah and not give way to those fears?*

ABRAHAM, ISAAC, AND JACOB

God often calls Himself the God of Abraham, Isaac, and Jacob. Why? In part, to show He is personal, but also to show He values us, not only for ourselves, but as golden links in a chain: He can see the generations to come.

Do you remember how God spoke to Cindy Baldwin when she was despairing about the way her son Matt was headed? She was weeping in her bedroom, literally down on her face, pounding her fists into the carpet when God spoke to her, His daughter, and said:

You are My heritage. You are My future. Matt is My child. You have to let go.

God took Abraham out and showed him the stars in the sky, saying, "so shall your descendants be." When Isaac proved to be a weak link in the chain, God provided Rebekah, because He cared about His *heritage*. When Rebekah took a wrong turn and led her son Jacob astray, God wooed Jacob, with a vision on a starry night, and then He refined him, taking him into the fire, wrestling with him in the desert. Why? Because Jacob was His *heritage*.

When Bob and Lori ran ahead of God and experienced pain, they did the wisest thing any of us can do. They fell on their faces. They repented of any known sin. They pleaded for God's help. When Jacob did that, God blessed him mightily. When the Becklers did that, God rewarded them with songs of deliverance—specifically, through Point of Grace!

Let me ask you: *Do you understand that God wants you to be pure because you are His heritage? Do you see yourself as a link in the chain, with a responsibility to be faithful to the next generation? If you are out of fellowship with God and He is contending with you, will you submit to Him? Will you allow Him to be Lord of every part of your life so that His Spirit may flow freely through you, dispensing joy, peace, and grace?*

THE HEBREW MIDWIVES AND JOCHEBED

God cared about His Heritage, so when they were in slavery and crying out to Him, He heard. In the opening of Exodus He used women mightily, and these women are part of our holy heritage. The Hebrew midwives and Jochebed proved themselves to be true daughters of Sarah by not giving way to hysterical fears but instead, putting their trust in God, and doing what was right. God used them to save lives, just as He is using Kathy Troccoli to save the lives of the unborn.

There are many ways to save lives. When we are alert to the people God puts in our path, reaching out with His love and His Word, we save lives. When we are faithful, as mothers and mentors, to teach the next generation the truths of the Lord, we save lives.

One way to do this is through seizing the teachable moments and by having family devotions. I remember one pastor saying, "It's a sin to make family devotions boring!" I don't know if I would go that far—but *why* have it be boring when it can be exciting? Skits are one of the best ways to bring life. Questions, following the skits, will help you delve into the meaning, including the hidden meanings, of our holy heritage. (Don't forget to avail yourself of these in Appendix B.)

Likewise, reading some of the great stories about heroes of the Christian faith can be a wonderful way to pass on the heritage and to save lives.

The real secret in being fruitful is abiding in Christ. When you do that, out of the overflow of your heart, the mouth will speak. Let me ask you: *Is Jesus your First Love? When you wake in the morning, do you run into His arms? Or do you put Him off, until the day has slipped away? When you are troubled, do you run to the throne—or do you run to the phone? Do you long to stay in the light of His favor? What do you talk about with the people in your life? Are you passing on the heritage so that the next generation will know?*

MIRIAM

Miriam certainly had a godly heritage. Even as a child she had been mentored and used of God to save her baby brother, Moses. She witnessed the miraculous plagues, and after she walked through the

Red Sea, she led all the women in a song of praise to God. Yet, she fell. God was angry with her and disciplined her by striking her with leprosy. Yet Moses and God also extended grace to her.

I am convinced that God is as concerned that we learn how to pass on grace as He is concerned that we pass on the stories that reflect His grace. It is costly to give grace, though it is free to the recipient. Think of what it cost Christ! How sad if we, who have been the recipients of so much grace, withhold it from one another. Miriam had been a slave as a child, and undoubtedly had feelings of degradation. Often when we get to know someone and see the pain in his or her past, we are more merciful. If we cannot forgive those who are repentant, might not God teach us, His *heritage*, a lesson to make us more compassionate?

Let me ask you this: *Do you show grace to those who have fallen? To those who have hurt you? Or do you want them to suffer? Is your home filled with grace notes? Is your family eager to be around you—or are they eager to flee?*

YOUR GRANDPARENTS AND PARENTS

If you *have* been blessed with godly parents or grandparents, as is the case with the Becklers and the Bowlings, then you need to capture that heritage. How? One way is to ask questions when you are together. Look at this pattern:

> *In the future, **when your son asks you**, "What is the meaning of the stipulations, decrees and laws the Lord our God has commanded you?" tell him: "We were slaves of Pharaoh in Egypt, but the Lord brought us out of Egypt with a mighty hand. Before our eyes the Lord sent miraculous signs and wonders—great and terrible—upon Egypt and Pharaoh and his whole household." (Deuteronomy 6:20-22)*

> ***And when your children ask you**, "What does this ceremony mean to you?" then tell them, "It is the Passover sacrifice to the Lord, who passed over the houses of the Israelites in Egypt and spared our homes when he struck down the Egyptians." (Exodus 12:26-27)*

Unless we ask questions of our grandparents, parents, aunts, and uncles—their precious experiences with God may never be passed to the next generation, but, instead, drop to the bottom of the river. Here are a few questions to ask at your next family gathering:

How did you come to put your faith in Christ?

Can you tell me about a time in your life when you were acutely aware of God's presence?

How have you grown closer to God?

What has He taught you in order to have victory over sin?

Why do we have the traditions or celebrations that we do? (For example, why did we use so many lights at Christmas? Why did we give something up during Lent?)

If you had your life to live over, what would you do differently?

So often when we get together we fail to talk about the things that really matter. We prepare the food, but not the soul food. On Thanksgiving we have a tradition of going around the table with this question: *What are you thankful for this year that you could not have been thankful for last year?* This year, our precious daughter-in-law, Julie, said:

The Lord has shown me how exciting and fulfilling it is to work in the area of my spiritual giftedness.[Julie's gift is administration.] *I absolutely loved organizing MOPS at our church and organizing the evangelistic Christmas tea. Sometimes people will ask me: "How can you stand making all those phone calls to find volunteers? Don't all the details for the food, the program, etc., drive you crazy?"*

I tell them, "Absolutely not. It makes my adrenaline flow because this is how the Lord has gifted me." I have also seen the absolute importance of prayer. With the Christmas tea we ran into conflict with another group in the church planning the Christmas musical, which was to occur the following weekend. We each had different ideas for how the lobby should be decorated. At first I was really upset—but I got down on my knees and

God impressed on my heart I should just let it go and submit, allowing the other group to decorate according to its plan. He gave me such a peace and it all fell together beautifully. Not only that, we had harmony within the church.

As we were passing the turkey and dressing, Julie was passing the soul food, not just to the next generation, but to all of us.

We also have a time of blessing one another. At birthdays, we each bless the birthday person. At Thanksgiving, everyone gets blessed by everyone. (Yes, it takes a long time, but nobody objects. It is a golden time.) For example:

Steve: *Let's bless Grandmother Brown.*

Anne: *Grandma—I think you are the best storyteller I've ever heard. I love it when you hold me and tell me a story.*

Sally: *You have a melody in your heart, Grandma—when you are cooking, when you are doing the backstroke in Green Bay, you are singing or humming—and you spread joy to all of us.*

This last Thanksgiving, when it was my turn to be blessed, my eighty-five-year-old father said, "With Dee Dee [his name for me], I've never had to doubt if I was loved."

I could hardly speak. My dad has trouble expressing emotion, but he did it. I will remember his kind words and the look in his eyes to my dying day. And it happened because we planned soul food, because we asked questions and had a time of blessing.

Let me ask you this: *If you have a godly heritage, are you seizing it while there is still time? Are you asking questions of the godly people in your life, discovering how God worked in their lives? Are you talking about spiritual things? Are you passing the soul food as well as the turkey and dressing?*

THE NEXT GENERATION

We also need to be telling our own stories. Over and over we've told our children the times when God's presence has been particularly real in our lives. Our two youngest children, who were both adopted from overseas orphanages, love the stories of how God led us to choose them. In addition to the big events in our lives (conversion, finding a marriage partner, deliverance from danger) there are all the little stories, the everyday ways we spy God.

Have you heard of the *God Hunt?* "The Chapel of the Air" initiated this popular spiritual discipline through its *50 Day Spiritual Adventure.* It encourages individuals to keep a journal on a daily basis, recording "God sightings." For example:

Did you have a specific answer to prayer?

Did God help you today in some specific way to do His work in the world?

Was there an unusual coincidence or timing that you suspect could have been designed by God?

Did God show you unusual mercy?

By being alert and keeping a journal, you are going to have "God sightings" to share at your family supper table. And so are the children! Our youngest, Annie, had lost a library book and did not want to pay for a new book. She hunted and hunted and was tearful about it. That night, before she went to sleep she prayed: *Jesus, please show me where I put that book.* That night she dreamed she saw the book on the third shelf of her bookcase, hidden behind a much bigger book. She woke up, ran to the third shelf and the big book—and voila! A God sighting. And a story to tell.

Our daughter-in-law, Julie, to whom I have dedicated my part of this book, is doing a wonderful job of keeping a record of answered prayers through her Creative Memories photo albums. When the children have an answer to prayer (such as when Emily prayed for a brother), Julie takes a picture and records the answer in an album she has called *The Against Forgetting Album.*

We also need the body of Christ to pass on the heritage: teachers, mentors, aunts, and uncles. This weekend some dear friends of ours, the Wilkinsons, invited us to their home for a bar mitzvah for their thirteen-year-old son, Nathaniel. The name comes from the Jewish ceremony in which a son is accepted into the congregation as a man. However, our friends are not Jewish. But they see great value in asking the body of believers to come and bless their son, on the threshold of manhood, with advice and prayers. (They did the same thing with their daughter a few years ago—Jews call that ceremony a bat mitzvah.) Included in the invitation were adults believers (and their children) who had been involved in some way in Nathaniel's life.

It was a meaningful night, passing down the *heritage* to Nathaniel and reminding us, as adults, of our responsibility to the next generation, the children God has put in our lives. After clinking our glasses of sparkling white grape juice and wishing Nathaniel a hearty "l'chaim!" (to your health!) we dined on poached pears, broasted chicken, and scalloped potatoes served on fine china. Then, each family or single adult offered blessings to Nathaniel.

One family read Psalm 1 and said they would be planting a tree in the yard in the spring. As it grew, Nathaniel was to remember that he, if he delighted in the Lord and His Word, could be like that tree, growing strong, able to withstand the trials of life, just as that tree would withstand the winds of Nebraska.

Nathaniel is an exceptionally talented and clever young boy.

At ten he could discuss politics intelligently, at eleven he could play a violin well, at twelve he could outwit the best of his teachers. All this giftedness could be used to serve God mightily, or it could turn out to be a weakness, if, like Jacob, he trusts in himself and not in God.

For our contribution to the bar mitzvah, my husband and I told Nathaniel he reminded us of Jacob, because of his cleverness and charm. Here, at the threshold of manhood, Nathaniel had a choice. He could either trust in himself, as Jacob did for the first forty years, and be refined by God, or he could see God as the awesome and sovereign God He truly is and give Him complete control.

Like the good sport (and ham) that he is, Nathaniel acted out the story with our coaching. After tricking his blind father, played by my husband, he fled for his life, running round and round the dining table. All forty guests sang "Jacob's Ladder" as Nathaniel pretended to sleep under the stars. Then Nathaniel is tricked into marrying homely Leah, played again by fun-loving husband Steve, who covered his face with a towel meant to resemble a heavy bridal veil.

Having a weekly family night is a good way to be intentional about passing on the heritage. Additional ideas for family nights can be found in the excellent Family Night Tool Chest series. (see Appendix C.)

Let me ask you this. *Are you telling your own stories of how God moved in your life? Are you recording them for future generations? Are you seizing opportunities at holidays or by making your own special traditions, to pass on the heritage? Do you have a weekly family night?*

EVEN THE CHILDREN YET TO BE BORN

God is still calling, still longing for us to embrace our holy heritage. Surely He called to the Bowlings and the Becklers on that Sunday when they were gathered for a family reunion and impressed Psalm 78 on their hearts as the backbone for Heritage Keepers. He is still blessing the Heritage Keepers conferences. He still calls to His daughters. He still longs for us to embrace our holy heritage, that the next generation will know. He is calling to you, He is calling to me:

> *My daughter, My daughter*
> *My precious child,*
> *I will open my mouth in parables,*
> *I will utter hidden things, things from of old—*
> *Tell them to your children, so the next generation would know them,*
> *even the children yet to be born and they in turn would tell their children.*
> *Then they would put their trust in God and would not forget his deeds.*

We give you our love, we ask you to go in peace, and to embrace, as we will, our holy heritage—that the next generation may know, even the children yet to be born.

Panning for Heritage Gold

☼ Icebreaker: In five years, what do you think you will remember from this book? Put your "take-away" in one sentence.

1. The message found in Psalm 78 can be found in many other places in Scripture, for it is so important to God.

    A. What similarities do you see in Psalm 77?

    B. What similarities do you see in Acts 7?

☀ You may want to turn back to earlier Bible studies to review your answers and the Scriptures.

2. What lessons has God impressed on your heart through the story of Eve?

3. As Satan tempted Eve, he will tempt you. How could you prepare yourself for his attacks?

4. Do you value your role as a mother or mentor? If so, give evidence.

5. Where is your focus? Are you distracted and worried about many things?

6. Do you and your family live a quiet life? If not, what changes could you make?

7. What do you remember from the marriage of Abraham and Sarah?

8. Are you working as a team with your husband, or, if you are single, with others in the body of Christ? Do you individually seek God's face and seek to be like-minded in Him? If not, what changes could you make?

9. What causes you fear and anxiety right now? Will you be a true daughter of Sarah and not give way to those fears?

10. What lessons has God impressed on your heart through His emphasis that He is the God of Abraham, Isaac, and Jacob—and that you are His heritage?

11. What do you remember from the life of Jacob?

12. What applications are there for you from Jacob?

13. If you are out of fellowship with God and He is contending with you, will you submit to Him? Why should you?

☀ 14. What will you remember from the lives of the Hebrew midwives?

What will you remember from Jochebed?

15. How have you demonstrated the kind of fruit that you saw in the above women?

16. Is Jesus your First Love? When you wake in the morning, do you run into His arms? Do you long to stay in the light of His favor? What does this tell you about yourself?

17. How are you passing on the heritage so that the next generation will know?

18. What will you remember from the life of Miriam?

19. Do you show grace to those who have fallen? To those who have hurt you? Give evidence.

20. Is your home filled with grace notes? Give evidence.

21. What are you doing to capture the stories of your immediate godly ancestors or mentors?

22. What are you doing to pass on your own stories to the next generation? Are you keeping records, establishing traditions, and telling stories? If not, what could you do differently?

PRAYER TIME:

Open your Bibles to Psalm 78 and pray through verses 1 through 8 together.

Have each woman lift up her own request and allow the others to support her with sentence prayers.

Appendix A

Helps for Preparation and Discussion of Bible Studies

Successful gold panning techniques:

1. Develop a habit of going down to the river of God's Word by choosing the same place and the same time each day. The study has been divided into three days, but each day could easily be divided again, making six quiet times.

2. Prepare your heart before you seek. Ask God to make you alert to the gold He has for you that day.

3. If you are not doing this study in a small group, still, make it a point to tell someone about the nugget you discovered. We remember best what we articulate ourselves.

Making your gold multiply in your small group:

1. Star the questions where you found nuggets. If you are naturally shy, ask God for courage to help you speak up. If you are naturally talkative, ask God for strength to be quiet when you do not have a star, so that others have time to share. If you didn't pan for gold, do not share unless everyone who did pan has been given the opportunity to share.

2. As God gives you discernment, make yourself vulnerable in your small group in discussion and prayer time. Gold is multiplied through honesty. Likewise, be faithful to the others, and keep their confidences. They have trusted you with gold.

Discussion leaders who facilitate panning:

1. Pray for your individual members. Put their names in a place you frequent often. Pray they will seek and that God will open their eyes to His gold.

2. Remember, the Holy Spirit is the teacher, and you are the facilitator. The Spirit will be prompting someone to answer, but if she is shy, she may need encouragement from you. "Anne, did you have something to share?"

2. Place the chairs in as small a circle as possible as space inhibits sharing.

3. Begin and end on time so that women will be punctual and will trust you to let them out as promised.

4. If you have a monopolizer who seems to be quenching the flow of discussion, here are some possible approaches:

> A. Pray for her. Often the too-talkative person has deep emotional needs.

> B. Ask, "Can we hear from someone whom we haven't heard from?"

> C. Try to sit next to, rather than across from her, as eye contact stimulates sharing.

> D. If the problem persists, be gentle but honest and direct. Take her aside and say something like, "I need your help so that the shyer members can share." That may be enough for her to respond, but if not, continue with: "Could you star a few questions and answer those, but hold back on the others? I love your insights, but I need your help so the shyer members have time to gather courage and speak up."

5. The main reason women drop out of a group is because they don't feel valued. Therefore:

> A. Pray for them individually, that the group will love them.

> B. Show them love with a warm greeting, affirmation when they share, and notes between meetings.

> C. Plan a social time for bonding, such as a luncheon. You could discuss an opening icebreaker at leisure.

Appendix B

Quick Skits for Passing on the Heritage

Directions:

Assign parts, get the props, and read the script aloud to your family. Then, except for the narrator, put the script aside and ad lib. The story doesn't need to be exact—just get the basics. One person may play more than one part. These skits, unless otherwise noted, will work for preschool and up. Discussion questions with stars are for preteens and up.

1. Father Abraham

Based on Genesis 15:4-6
All sing "Father Abraham Had Many Sons"
Parts: Narrator, Voice of the Lord, Abraham
Props: Stars—if they are out, go outside—otherwise, pretend!

Narrator: *The word of the Lord came to Abraham and the Lord took Abraham outside.*

Voice of the Lord: *Look up into the heavens and count the stars if you can.*

Abraham: (Looks up and is amazed.)

Voice of the Lord: *Your descendants will be like that—too many to count!*

Narrator: *Abraham believed God and the Lord declared him righteous because of his faith.*

Discussion Questions:

1. Why did God take Abraham outside and what did He say to him?

2. What point was God making?

3. How did Abraham respond?

4. What pleased God about Abraham?

5. God is pleased when we have faith in His Word. Name one promise of God you believe.

*6. Abraham was a spiritual giant. There is an attractiveness in men like this that makes other men not so intriguing. Will you be this kind of man or woman? If so, what will help you to become strong?

2. A Bride for Isaac
Based on Genesis 24
Parts: Narrator, Abraham, Servant, Rebekah
Props: Jewelry the servant brings; a large pitcher for Rebekah

Narrator: *Abraham was an old man and the Lord had blessed him in every way. Abraham's son, Isaac, was forty, and he did not have a wife.*

Abraham: *My dear servant, come here.*

Servant: (Bows down.)

Abraham: *I want you to find a bride for my son Isaac—and I want you to promise me, before God, you will not get a bride from here—from these unbelieving Canaanites.*

Servant: *I promise.*

Abraham: *Go to my country and find a wife from my relatives.*

Servant: *But what if she won't come back with me?*

Abraham: *God has made promises to me, and I believe Him. God will send an angel before you to help you.*

Servant: (Takes jewelry from Abraham and then goes out to the barn and saddles up ten camels. He and the ten camels walk a long, long way—all around the room many times. Then they finally arrive at Abraham's country and stop by the well. The servant bows down and prays:) *O Lord, God of my master Abraham, give me success today. As the daughters of the townspeople are coming out to draw water, show me the one* who is to marry my master's son, Isaac. When I say, "Please let me have a drink from your jar," let her say: "Drink, and I will water your camels too." Let this be a sign to me that she is the one.

Narrator: *Before the servant had even finished praying, a beautiful virgin, Rebekah, came.*

Servant: *Please let me have a drink.*

Rebekah: *Drink, and I will water your camels as well.* (She runs to fill the pitcher at the well, again and again, and then runs to fill the trough where the camels are drinking.)

Servant: *You are the one! God has sent his angel before me and shown me! This jewelry is a gift from your future husband.* (The servant bows down and worships the Lord, giving thanks. Then he rises and says:) *Let's go tell what has happened to your family!*

Narrator: *They run to Rebekah's home, tell the story, and Rebekah, in faith, like Abraham, leaves her family to obey God and to become the bride of Isaac.*

Discussion Questions

1. What did Abraham make his servant promise? Why, do you think?

*2. What are some of the reasons God would not want a believer and an unbeliever to marry?

*3. What are some ways to make sure that, if you marry, you marry a believer?

4. Why did Abraham believe that his servant would be able to find a bride for his son Isaac?

*5. How can a godly parent help to find God's choice for his child's mate?

6. How many camels did the servant take? What else did he take? When he came, what do you think the people in the town thought?

7. How did the servant pray? How did God answer?

*8. The servant "threw out a fleece." Explain what that is according to Judges 6:36-40.

*9. Some feel that now that we have God's Word and the Holy Spirit, asking for a specific sign, "a fleece," is inappropriate. Others feel that if you do "throw out a fleece," it should be so specific that it could not possibly be answered by coincidence, and it should only be done for positive affirmations, for a negative response may simply mean God has chosen not to answer you through a fleece. What do you think?

10. How did the servant respond when God answered his prayer?

11. Think of a time when God answered your prayer. How did you respond?

*12. Rebekah has been compared to Abraham. What similarities do you see?

13. How seriously did the servant take the job Abraham had given him? How seriously do you take the jobs given to you by parents or teachers?

3. Battling Brothers: Jacob and Esau
(May be too mature for very young children)
Based on Genesis 25:21-28
Parts: Narrator, Voice of the Lord, Rebekah
Props: Two pillows

Narrator: *For twenty years Rebekah wanted a baby, but God didn't give her one. Finally, her husband, Isaac, prayed for his wife to be able to have babies, and the Lord answered his prayer by giving her twins. She had two babies in her womb. But while they were inside of her, they were fighting. They wrestled, they knocked their heads together—and Rebekah was miserable.*

Rebekah: (Has two pillows under her shirt. With difficulty, she kneels down to pray.) *Lord, I am so miserable. I don't know what is happening. It is like this baby is jumping up and down—tell me, Lord—what is happening?*

Voice of the Lord: *Two nations are in your womb, and two peoples from within you will be separated; one people will be stronger than the other, and the older will serve the younger.*

Narrator: *Rebekah gave birth to twin boys, and when they were born, Jacob was grasping Esau's heel. Each parent had a favorite child. Isaac loved Esau the best because they both liked to hunt. Rebekah loved Jacob the best because they were both liked to stay quietly at home. It hurt the boys that each parent had a favorite. The boys did not get along.*

Discussion Questions

1. Why did Isaac pray? How did God answer?

2. Why was Rebekah so miserable? What did she do about it?

*3. What did God tell her? What did it mean?

*4. What hurtful thing did the mother and father do?

Sometimes a child will be shown favor for a short period of time, because of need or circumstances. But if a parent has a favorite child over a lifetime, it brings harm to the whole family. Why?

5. How have your parents shown you that they value you?

Close with a time of prayer by having each person lift a need in prayer and the others support him or her with a sentence. Encourage prayer for character as well as other needs. For example:

> Mom: Please help me to love You more, Jesus.
> Tommy: Yes, Lord, please give Mom more love for You.
> Dad: I agree, Lord.

4. The Dirty Trick of Rebekah and Jacob
(May be too mature for very young children)
Based on Genesis 27
Parts: Narrator, Rebekah, Jacob, Isaac, and Esau
Props: A stuffed animal, a bowl, and a sweater

Narrator: *In the Bible, when a man was very old and thought he might die soon, he called for all his children and grandchildren and said a prayer for each of them. There was a special prayer for the firstborn son, which God honored. Isaac was old and nearly blind, but he didn't call for both his sons, because he* liked Esau best. So he called for just Esau. Rebekah, however, is standing outside the door, eavesdropping.

Isaac: *Ah, my favorite son. I may be going to die soon so I want to bless you. But first, go kill a goat and get me a tasty bowl of goat stew. Then I will bless just you.* (Esau runs off, not seeing his mother.)

Rebekah: *Jacob! Jacob! Listen carefully. Go and kill a goat quickly, and I will quickly make stew for your father. I want you to pretend to be your brother Esau.* (Jacob runs and kills a goat. He puts a sweater on, to resemble a goat skin.)

Jacob: *My father.*

Isaac: *Yes, my son. Who is it?*

Jacob: *I am your firstborn, Esau. I have done what you asked. Please sit up and give me your blessing.*

Isaac: *How did you do it so quickly?*

Jacob: *The Lord your God gave me success.*

Isaac: *Come near so I can touch you to see if you are really Esau.* (Jacob comes near and Isaac feels his sweater.)

Isaac: *Ah, my son Esau. I will bless you. "May nations serve you—may you be lord over your brothers. May those who curse you be cursed and those who bless you be blessed."* (Isaac leaves. A short time later, Esau enters with a bowl.)

Esau: *Father, I have done as you asked. Please sit up and give me your blessing.*

Isaac: *But I already gave you my blessing. Who are you?*

Esau: *I am Esau, your firstborn! Bless me, oh my father, bless me!*

Isaac: *It is too late! Jacob came deceitfully, pretending to be you, and stole the blessing that belonged to you.*

Esau: (Running out in anguish) *I hate my brother. When my father dies, I will kill him!*

Rebekah: *Jacob! Jacob! Your brother is very angry. Run, run—to my brother*

Laban's home far away. I will call for you when your brother calms down. (Jacob flees for his life.)

Discussion Questions

1. Isaac, Rebekah, and Jacob all did things that were very wrong. What were they and why were they wrong?

2. What pain did their sin bring to others?

3. What pain did their sin bring to themselves?

4. In what situations are people tempted to lie and cheat? Why do they do it?

5. Why is their thinking foolish?

6. Close by having each parent bless each child. Bless them with physical touch (place your hands on their shoulders—or hold the child), telling the children something you value in them.

5. Jacob's Ladder
Based on Genesis 28:10-22
Parts: Narrator, Jacob, Voice of the Lord, optional angels
Props: Fabric stretching out to be a ladder (a floor-length drapery, a sheet tucked over the top of a door)

Narrator: *Jacob ran and ran away from home, away from his brother's anger. Weary, he lay down and used a stone for a pillow. While he slept, he had a dream in which he saw a stairway resting on the earth with its top reaching to heaven, and the angels of God ascending and descending on it.*

Jacob: (Runs and sleeps—looks toward the ladder where optional angels are standing with outstretched wings. If you family knows the song "Jacob's Ladder" or "Our God Is an Awesome God," sing it.)

Voice of the Lord: *I am the Lord, the God of your father Abraham and the God of Isaac. I will give you and your descendants the land on which you are lying. Your descendants will be like the dust of the earth. All peoples will be blessed* through you and your offspring. I am with you and will watch over you wherever you go, and I will bring you back to this land.

Jacob: (Wakes up and says:) *Surely the Lord was in this place. How awesome is this place.* (Stands and stretches.) *If God will be with me and if He will watch over me and if He will bring me back safely to my father's house, then the Lord will be my God. Why, I'll even tithe!*

Discussion Questions

1. Describe the dream Jacob had and what God told him.

2. What did Jacob say when he woke up?

3. Should God be our God only if He does good things for us? Why or why not?

4. What do you think Jacob still had to learn about God?

6. Laban's Dirty Trick
Based on Genesis 29:16-30
Parts: Narrator, Jacob, Rachel, Laban, and Leah
Props: A towel for Leah's veil

Narrator: *When Jacob arrived at his Uncle Laban's ranch he met beautiful Rachel and fell in love with her.*

Jacob: *Oh Rachel, beautiful Rachel!* (He kisses her.)

Narrator: *Rachel's father, Laban, was a tricky guy.*

Jacob: *Oh Laban, I will work for you for seven years if you let me marry your beautiful younger daughter Rachel.*

Laban: *Good idea! Work for me for seven years and then I will let you marry her.*

Narrator: *Jacob works hard for seven years. That night, he thinks he is going to marry Rachel, but Laban is going to trick him. Laban puts a veil over his homely older daughter Leah.*

Laban: *Leah, my dear, pretend you are Rachel.*

Leah: *Okay, Dad.*

Narrator: *So that night Jacob and Leah were married—but Jacob thought he was marrying Rachel. The next morning, when it was light—Jacob realized he had been tricked. He ran out of his tent and grabbed Laban.*

Jacob: *What is this you have done to me? I worked seven years for Rachel!*

Laban: (Smiling) *Calm down. I'll let you marry Rachel too. Just work for me for another seven years.*

Jacob: *ARGHHHHHHHHH!*

Discussion Questions

1. How did Laban deceive Jacob?

2. Why do you think Laban lied?

3. How did this lie hurt Jacob? Rachel? Leah? Laban?

3. Sometimes a lie seems like the easy way out. Why isn't it?

4. Sometimes God allows us to be hurt the way we have hurt others so that we can become more compassionate. How was Jacob hurt the way he had hurt others?

7. A Faithful Big Sister
Based on Exodus 2:1-10
Parts: Narrator, Jochebed, Miriam, Princess, an optional crocodile
Props: A doll in a basket, a blue sheet or blanket to be the river

Narrator: *God's people were slaves in Egypt, and the king was very cruel to them. He was also afraid of them, because there were so many of them. So the bad king tried to think of ways to get rid of the baby boys. If one of God's people had a baby boy, he told the soldiers to find it and throw the baby into the river. Jochebed had a baby boy named Moses.*

Jochebed: (Holding doll) *Oh, Miriam, I need you to keep your little baby brother quiet. Rock him, and hide with him in the closet.* (Hands baby to Miriam)

Miriam: (Does as told)

Jochebed: *Oh, Miriam, I need you to help me make a basket for your brother. Help me coat it with tar to keep water out.*

Miriam: (Does as told)

Jochebed: *Oh, Miriam. Come with me down to the Nile. Let us pray: "Dear Lord, please protect Moses and save him." Oh, Miriam, if God answers our prayers and the princess finds your little brother in the basket, ask her if she would like someone to take care of him for her. Then run and get me.*

Miriam. *Yes, Mother.*

Narrator: *God watched over Moses. He floated right by the crocodile, but the crocodile did not hurt him. He floated right down to the palace just as the princess was coming down to bathe.*

Princess: *I hear a baby crying!* (Opens the basket) *Oh, how precious. This must be one of the Hebrew babies. I will adopt him.*

Miriam: (Suddenly appearing) *Would you like me to find a Hebrew woman to take care of him?*

Princess: *Yes, go get her. I will pay her!*

Narrator: *Miriam runs and runs, full of joy that God has answered prayer, to get her mother.*

Miriam: *Mother—God has answered our prayers. The princess found Moses and wants you to take care of him!*

Discussion Questions
1. What frightening situation did the family of Miriam face?

2. How did they turn to God?

3. How was Miriam pleasing to God?

4. How did God answer their prayers?

5. Is there a situation that makes you afraid right now?

6. What did you learn from this story that might help you?

Appendix C

Books and Tapes for Passing on the Heritage

These are Dee's 'cream of the crop' recommendations.

Preschool:
Read-Aloud Bible Stories (all volumes) by Ella K. Lindvall, illustrations by H. Kent Puckett. These are, in my opinion, without equal for small children.

Lower Elementary:
Little Visits with God (ages 4-8) by Allan Hart Jahsmann

Middle Elementary School and Up:
The Narnia Series by C.S. Lewis
Read these with your children and help them to see "the hidden pictures." How is Aslan like Jesus? How are we like the children? A Focus on the Family Radio Theater production of *The Lion, the Witch and the Wardrobe* is available on audiocassette or CD: 1-800-A-FAMILY.

Pilgrim's Progress by John Bunyan—*Dangerous Journey*, a beautiful version of *Pilgrim's Progress*, is available in both book and video. The video can be obtained through Gateway Video: 1-800-523-0226.

Junior High School, High School, and Adult
Biographies of believers in recent history can help young people, and ourselves, desire to live wholeheartedly for Christ.

The Shadow of the Almighty by Elisabeth Elliot
The martyrdom of five young missionaries.

Chasing the Dragon by Jackie Pullinger with Andrew Quicke
The story of Jackie Pullinger, whom God called, at the age of twenty, to Hong Kong's infamous walled city of addicts and prostitutes.

The Cross and the Switchblade by David Wilkerson
The story of David Wilkerson, and how God used him with gangs in New York City. (Also available in video.)

The Cost of Discipleship by Dietrich Bonhoeffer
A powerful statement of the demands of sacrifice from a man who opposed the Nazis and was hung by the Gestapo. A Focus on the Family Radio Theater production of *Bonhoeffer: The Cost of Freedom* is available on audiocassette or CD: 1-800-A-FAMILY.

The Hiding Place by Corrie ten Boom
The story of how God used a family to hide Jews during World War II. (Also available in video.)

No Compromise by Melodie Green
The story of Keith Green, songwriter and singer.

Families
Family Night Tool Chest series by Jim Weidmann and Kurt Bruner:
Introduction to Family Nights
Basic Christian Beliefs
Christian Character Qualities
and more ...

This series will give you more ideas for creative family nights that pass down the heritage.

Endnotes

Chapter Two: *I Will Show You Hidden Things*

1. Charles Spurgeon, *The Treasury of David*, vol. 3 (Peabody, MA: Hendrickson, n.d.), 2.

2. Charles Spurgeon, 2.

3. Charles Spurgeon, *The Treasury of David*, vol. 2 (Peabody, MA: Hendrickson, n.d.), 366.

4. Walter Wangerin, Jr., *The Book of God: The Bible as a Novel* (Grand Rapids, MI: Zondervan, 1996), 19-20.

5. Gordon J. Wenham, *Word Biblical Commentary*, eds. David A. Hubbard, Glenn W. Barker, and John D. W. Watts, "Genesis 16-50," vol. 2 (Dallas: Word, 1994), 85.

Chapter Three: *A Snake in the Grass*

1. C.S. Lewis, *The Lion, the Witch and the Wardrobe* (New York: Harper Trophy, 1978), 32-33.

2. Gordon J. Wenham, *Word Biblical Commentary*, eds. David A. Hubbard, Glenn W. Barker, and John D. W. Watts, "Genesis 1-15," vol. 1 (Dallas: Word, 1987), 57.

3. Beth Moore, *Broken Hearts, Broken Ties*, videotape (Nashville: Lifeway, 1995).

4. Burt Curtis and John Eldredge, *The Sacred Romance: Drawing Closer to the Heart of God* (Nashville: Thomas Nelson, 1997), 14.

5. Gordon J. Wenham, vol. 1, 106.

6. Gordon J. Wenham, vol. 2, 7.

Chapter Four: *A Heritage of Harmony*

1. G. von Rad, as quoted in Gordon J. Wenham, vol. 1, 83.

Chapter Five: *We Need to be Heritage Keepers!*

1. Charles Spurgeon, vol. 2, 366.

2. D. Kidner, as quoted in Marvin E. Tate, *Word Biblical Commentary*, eds. David A. Hubbard, Glenn W. Barker and John D. W. Watts, "Psalms 51-100," vol. 20 (Dallas: Word, 1990), 295.

3. Charles Spurgeon, vol. 2, 331.

Chapter Six: *Daughters of Sarah*

1. Tertullian, as quoted in Herbert B. Workman, *Persecution in the Early Church* (Oxford, England: University Press, 1980), 117, 143.

2. Tacitus, as quoted in *1 Peter James: Living Through Difficult Times*, Serendipity Group Bible Study (Littleton, CO: Serendipity, 1995), 8.

3. A Baby's Prayer Foundation, PO Box 1458, Jupiter, FL 33468, 888-673-4273, www.abpf.org.

4. Kathy Troccoli, *My Life Is in Your Hands* (Grand Rapids, MI: Zondervan, 1997), 104.

5. Holt International Children's Services, PO Box 2880, Eugene, OR 97402, 541-687-2202, www.holtintl.org

6. Jane Hansen, *Fashioned for Intimacy* (Ventura, CA: Regal, 1997), 91.

7. Jane Hansen, 91.

8. Gary Smalley and John Trent, *The Language of Love* (Pomona, CA: Focus on the Family, 1988), 9.

9. Gordon J. Wenham, vol. 2, 48.

Chapter Seven: *Stay in Step with the Spirit*

1. Neil T. Anderson, *Victory over the Darkness* (Ventura, CA: Regal, 1990), 101.

2. Gordon J. Wenham, vol. 2, 138.

3. Gordon J. Wenham, vol. 2, 149.

4. Point of Grace with Davin Seay, *Life, Love, and Other Mysteries* (New York: Pocket, 1996), 49.

5. Gordon J. Wenham, vol. 2, 155.

6. Elise Arndt, *A Mother's Touch* (Wheaton, IL: Victor, 1983), 126.

7. Neil T. Anderson, 98.

8. Neil T. Anderson, 104.

Chapter Eight: *Point of Grace: Passing on a Godly Heritage*

1. Point of Grace, 7.

2. Fritz Ridenour, *It's Your Move* (Glendale, CA: Regal, 1970), 30.

3. Leslie Williams, *Night Wrestling: Struggling for Answers and Finding God* (Dallas: Word, 1997), 14.

4. Charles Spurgeon, vol. 2, 364.

5. Charles Spurgeon, vol. 2, 279.

6. Ruth Bell Graham, as quoted in *Experiencing God's Presence*, by Janet Kobobel Grant, ed. Traci Mullins (Grand Rapids, MI: Zondervan, 1998), 50.

Chapter Nine: *Kathy Troccoli: A Single Woman Passing on the Heritage*

1. Kathy Troccoli, back cover.

2. *The Visual Bible: The Healing Touch of Jesus* videotape (Dallas: Visual Entertainment, Inc., 1997).

3. Luci Shaw, *Water My Soul: Cultivating the Interior Life* (Grand Rapids: Zondervan, 1998), 88-89.

4. "A Baby's Prayer," Copyright © 1996 Sony/ATV Songs LLC, Sony/ATV Tunes LLC and Molto Bravo Music, Inc. All rights administered by Sony/ATV Music Publishing, 8 Music Square West, Nashville, TN 37203. All rights reserved, used by permission.

5. Kathy Troccoli, 103.

6. George Rawlinson, *The Pulpit Commentary*, eds. H. D. M. Spence and Joseph S. Exell, "Exodus." vol. 1 (Peabody, MA: Hendrickson, n.d.), 17.

Chapter Ten: *Sandi Patty: Passing on a Heritage of Grace*

1. Philip Yancey, *What's So Amazing About Grace?* (Grand Rapids, MI: Zondervan, 1997), 79.

2. Jennie Dimkoff, "Choosing to Trust," cassette tape (Fremont, MI: n.d.)

3. George Rawlinson, 34.

4. George Rawlinson, 24.

5. Sandi Patty, as quoted in *What My Parents Did Right*, ed. Gloria Gaither (Nashville: StarSong, 1991), 177.

6. Os Guinness, *The Call: Finding and Fulfilling the Central Purpose of Your Life* (Nashville: Word, 1998), 118.

7. ABC News, *PrimeTime Live*, "A Song and a Prayer" (New York, Dec. 3, 1997).

8. Philip Yancey, 100.

9. Greg Johnson and Mike Yorkey, *Faithful Parents, Faithful Kids* (Wheaton, IL: Tyndale, 1993), 20.

Chapter Eleven: *Against Forgetting*

1. Charles Spurgeon, vol. 2, 363.

2. Charles Spurgeon, vol. 2, 337.

3. Peter Marshall, *Mr. Jones, Meet the Master: Sermons and Prayers of Peter Marshall*, ed. Catherine Marshall (Grand Rapids, MI: Revell, 1982), 147-149.

For more information on Heritage Keepers Conferences or video
call 1-800-497-2660 or see www.HeritageKeepers.com